THE JHELUM

A Victorian Merchant Ship

Michael Stammers and John Kearon

ALAN SUTTON

NATIONAL MUSEUMS & GALLERIES
ON MERSEYSIDE

First published in the United Kingdom in 1992 by
Alan Sutton Publishing Ltd · Phoenix Mill · Far Thrupp · Stroud · Gloucestershire
in association with
Trustees of the National Museums and Galleries on Merseyside

First published in the United States of America in 1993 by
Alan Sutton Publishing Inc. · Wolfeboro Falls · NH 03896–0848

British Library Cataloguing in Publication Data

Stammers, M.K.
  "Jhelum": Victorian Merchant Ship
  I. Title II. Kearon, John
  387.2

  ISBN 0–7509–0230–2

Library of Congress Cataloging in Publication Data

Stammers, Michael.
  The Jhelum: a Victorian merchant ship/by Michael Stammers and John Kearon.
    p. cm.
  Includes bibliographical references
  ISBN 0–7509–0230–2
  1. Jhelum (Ship) I. Kearon, John, 1946–. II. Title.
  VM395.J46S73 1992
  387.2'24–dc20

                                         92–27460
                                             CIP

Cover illustration: The Jhelum, *bow view (Trustees of the National Museum and Galleries on Merseyside).*

Typeset in 10/12 Bembo.
Typesetting and origination by
Alan Sutton Publishing Limited.
Printed in Great Britain by
The Bath Press, Bath, Avon.

To John Smith, MBE, FRGS,
Curator of the Falklands Museum, Stanley,
and a good friend

The three-masted wooden square-rigged sailing ship was probably the most important vehicle in human history.

Its invention in the shadows of the 15th century opened up the world to the economic and political domination of northern Europe. . . . This dominance lasted until 1870 when the capabilities of the wooden three-masted square-rigged vessel were outrun by the industrial conditions it had played such a part in creating.

G. Kahre (B. Greenhill, ed.), *The Last Tall Ships,* London, 1978, p. 15

The *Jhelum* and the Merseyside Maritime Museum team in January 1987, (left to right) Jim Forrester, John Kearon, Mike Stammers (Paul Browne took the photograph).

CONTENTS

ACKNOWLEDGEMENTS

The authors gratefully acknowledge the help of the following institutions and individuals for supplying and giving permission to reproduce illustrations: Trustees of the National Museum and Galleries on Merseyside, pp. iv, 12, 18, 23, 54, 55, 56, 58, 59, 60, 63, 64, 65, 66, 67, 68, 69, 70, 74, 76, 77, 78, 79, 80, 83, 84, 86, 87, 90, 93, 96, 97, 100, 101, 102, 103, 105, 106, 110, 114, 115, 116, 117, 119; Mr Anthony Steel, p. 20; Mr Sidney Beaglehole, p. 39; Miss Madge Biggs, MBE, p. 43; Southampton Maritime Museum, p. 52; Mr Karl Kortum, pp. 73, 88; Mr Jim Elliot, p. 111; the King's Regiment , p. 118.

CHAPTER ONE

INTRODUCTION

The expansion of world trade led by the United Kingdom in the mid-19th century was remarkable for its speed; estimates suggest that it grew between 5.6 and 4.8 per cent per annum between 1840 and 1860.[1] Liverpool was a major participant in this phenomenon, becoming the premier British port for exports. By 1857 its share of British exports was 45 per cent, compared with London's 23 per cent.[2] It was the chief emporium for cotton in the world, importing 365,000 tons of a British total of 395,000 tons in 1852.[3] Trading connections were expanded beyond the Atlantic basin to India, China, Australia and the west coast of the Americas. The docks were rebuilt and expanded to cope with the increase in traffic and included innovative specialist berths for imports such as the Albert, Stanley and Wapping Docks with their bonded public warehousing constructed on the quayside.

The cargoes were still carried mainly in wooden sailing ships; steamers were to be found on coastal packet services and subsidised long-distance mail runs. Most ships were British-owned but there was a substantial American presence, especially in the North Atlantic trade. Their design and size changed slowly between 1800 and 1849. This was largely because of the protection from foreign shipbuilders and ships afforded by the Navigation Acts and the restrictions imposed by the method of measuring tonnage. There was a substantial fleet of locally owned ships which totalled 573 vessels (over 100 tons) by 1854. Its average tonnage had increased to 444 tons as against 233 tons in 1829–35.[4]

Whereas British shipbuilders seem to have supplied most ships in the 18th century, demand increased at 4 per cent per annum between 1820 and 1850, outstripping supply. By 1846, 20 per cent of the British fleet had been built in British North America. These ships were substantially cheaper than British-built ones, but were considered of lesser quality, being built of inferior 'softwoods'. Liverpool was the biggest centre for their import and by 1846 they accounted for between 50 and 60 per cent of locally registered vessels.[5] The local shipbuilders who had supplied local demand in the 18th century were eventually either closed down by this competition and that of the British shipbuilding centres of the Clyde, Tyne and Wear or made the transition to building iron-hulled steam and sailing vessels.

It was against this background that the *Jhelum*, a wooden three-masted ship, was launched at Liverpool in 1849. Her shipbuilder-merchant owners ran her mainly to the west coast of South America, carrying general cargo out and copper, nitrates and wool homeward until 1863. She was then sold and continued trading mainly with coal cargoes outward and guano homewards on the same route. She had made

eighteen round voyages and was on her nineteenth when she put into Stanley in the
Falkland Islands in a sinking condition in August 1870. After a long delay she was
formally abandoned in 1871 and converted into a storage hulk. Her remains lie in the
harbour of Stanley, the principal town of the Falklands, at the head of Packe's Jetty
and opposite the Colonial Secretary's residence, Sulivan House. She is no longer used
for storage and lies abandoned, derelict and deteriorating. This book examines her history, design and construction through research in documentary sources and archaeological fieldwork.

The *Jhelum* lies in the Falklands because the islands' position – some five hundred
miles to the north of Cape Horn – made them a refuge for storm-battered sailing vessels making the passage from the Atlantic to the Pacific or vice versa. The seas at the
extreme south of South America are an area of violent storms, huge waves and ice-
bergs. Many sailing ships had to brave their treacherous waters to make passage to and
from the west coast of North and South America and from Australia and the Pacific
Islands. When the Falklands became a British possession, Stanley was set up as the capital and as a harbour of refuge with repair facilities. However, repairs in this remote
part of the world were expensive. Sometimes the owners of damaged vessels could not
afford the cost and as a result their ships were condemned as unseaworthy and sold off.
Some, like the *Jhelum* and the famous *Great Britain*, were converted for use as storage
hulks. Anchored in the harbour or beached at the end of long jetties, they provided a
convenient landing and storage place for local wool exports, imported goods, and for
the temporary warehousing of cargoes of ships undergoing repairs.

This book is divided into two parts: a history of the ship from 1849 to 1871 and a
report on the investigation of her hulk and the 'first aid' stabilisation programme carried out between 1987 and 1990. The first part contains sections on her builders, her
management and operation, her captains and crews, and her last voyage. The second
part includes a detailed description of all parts of her surviving hulk with some discus-
sion of particularly significant features, earlier surveys and the techniques used to carry
out the work. The bulk of the fieldwork was carried out between 1987 and 1990 in
three two-week periods and I must thank my colleagues John Kearon, Jim Forrester
and Paul Browne for their fortitude in what was a very intensive programme in often
difficult conditions. John was mainly responsible for the measured surveys and drawing up the plans back in Liverpool, and also contributed to chapters 6 to 14. Jim took
charge of logistics and the stabilisation programme, and Paul (in November 1987) provided us with a detailed photographic record and extensive video footage.

We must thank the following people and institutions for their contribution to the
project: His Excellency the Governor of the Falkland Islands, William Fullerton,
CMG; Mr Ronald Sampson, Chief Executive of the Falkland Islands Government;
Councillor Norma Edwards, Chair of the Falkland Islands Historic Wrecks and Hulks
Advisory Committee; Mr John Smith, MBE, FRGS, Curator of the Falkland Islands
Museum, Miss Jane Cameron, the Government archivist; Mr Terry Spruce, manager
of the Falkland Islands Company, for access to the FIC records; Mrs Joan Spruce, JP,
Chairman of the Falkland Islands Museum Committee; Mr Les Halliday, Registrar of
Shipping and Harbour Master at Stanley; Mr David Eynon of South Atlantic Marine
Services; Miss Madge Biggs, MBE, for permission to use the photograph taken in
1871 by her grandfather, Mr William Biggs; the Falklands Conservation (formerly the

Falkland Islands Trust) for a grant towards the work in 1990; the volunteers of 1st Battalion, the King's Regiment, and Operation Raleigh (Stanley group); Miss Sukey Cameron and the Falkland Islands London office staff; Mr Anthony Steel, Dr John Seymour and Mr Sydney Beaglehole for information about their ancestors; Mr David MacGregor for valuable advice and comments; and my secretary, Mrs Julie Stanley, who has not only coped with M.K. Stammers's writing but read the proofs of this work.

Notes

1. J.R. Hanson, *Trade in Transition* (London, 1980), pp. 13–14.
2. F.E. Hyde, 'The Growth of Liverpool's Trade 1700–1950', in *A Scientific Survey of Merseyside*, ed. W. Smith (Liverpool, 1953), pp. 159–60.
3. B. Poole, *The Commerce of Liverpool* (London and Liverpool, 1854), p. 2.
4. M.K. Stammers, 'The Jhelum and Liverpool Shipbuilders', in *Liverpool Shipping, Trade and Industry*, ed. V. Burton (Liverpool, 1989), p. 83.
5. E.W. Sagar with G. Panting, *Maritime Capital, the Shipping Industry in Atlantic Canada, 1820–1914* (Montreal, 1990), pp. 33–4.

PART ONE

A HISTORY OF THE *JHELUM*
1849–71

CHAPTER TWO

BUILDING THE *JHELUM*

Joseph Steel & Son launched the *Jhelum*, a wooden three-masted, full-rigged ship, at Liverpool on 24th May 1849.[1] Joseph Steel the elder was born in 1780 and died at Liverpool in November 1854. He started the firm at Liverpool in 1831. Family tradition has it that he originally came from Scotland and worked in one of the Cumbrian ports, probably Whitehaven, before settling in Liverpool.[2] His son, also named Joseph, became a partner in 1839. They built twenty-seven wooden merchant sailing ships between 1831 and 1859 at a rate of about one a year, starting with the *Cordelia* of 370 tons and ending with the *Mary Ellen* of 110 tons.[3] No ships were launched in 1837, 1838, 1850, 1853 and 1857 and it is likely that the business repaired ships in the public graving docks of the port at Canning, Queen's, Brunswick and Clarence Docks.

Thirteen ships were built for eight Liverpool owners: Taylor, Potter & Co had six; Barton, Irlam & Higginson had two; and John Bibby, Job Brothers (noted whale-oil and seal-skin merchants with a base in Newfoundland), J. Mondel and Captain B. Sproutz, Thomas Harrison (the West African merchant and associate of James Baines & Co), and Gladstone & Co had one each. It is not clear for whom the barque *Faerie Queen* was built in 1833. It is assumed that her owner did not come from Liverpool. The remaining 14 were built by Steel to trade on its own account, starting with the appropriately named *Enterprise* (338 tons) in 1835, and from 1845 to 1859 only two ships were built for outside customers. The ships conformed to the average size of Liverpool and British ships of the period and followed the trend to increased size that became increasingly evident after 1850. The biggest were the *Grand Bonny* (701 tons), built in 1852 for Thomas Harrison, and the *Joseph Steel* (900 tons), built in 1854, and the *Agra* (829 tons) built in 1858 for Steel. The *Jhelum* was twelfth in size.

The Steel yard was on the northern bank of the Mersey, sandwiched between the shore and Queen's Graving Docks. The address was Baffin Street, recalling the Arctic whalers that formerly berthed in Queen's Dock. Two more shipyards, Royden and Chaloner, were its northern neighbours and a dock for Mersey flats, Eagle Basin, was to the south. The yard had a river frontage of 116 feet with a small inlet at its centre and measured 400 feet inland to Baffin Street. Most of the site was open ground for timber storage with two building berths, one for ships of 600–700 tons and the other for those of 200 tons.[4] A plan dated 1841 from an unknown source in A.R. Burstall's pamphlet on Liverpool shipbuilding showed four buildings at the inland end of the site.[5] Joseph Steel junior probably gave up the yard in 1859 and it was taken on by W.H. Potter & Co in 1860.[6] Potter retained Steel's buildings and they could be seen on the aerial view of Liverpool commissioned by the *Illustrated London News* in 1865.

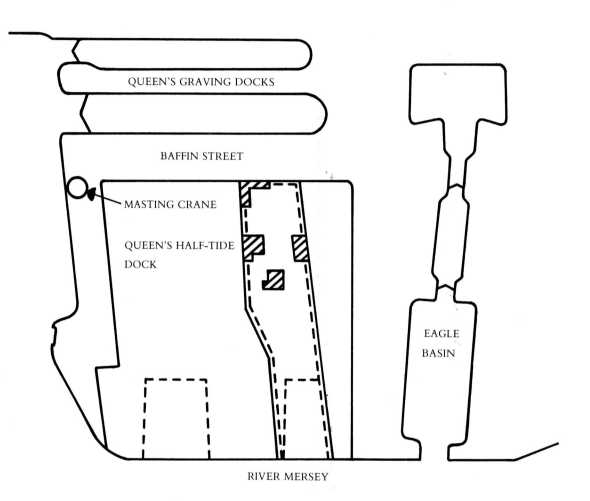

QUEEN'S DOCK

QUEEN'S GRAVING DOCKS

BAFFIN STREET

MASTING CRANE

QUEEN'S HALF-TIDE
DOCK

EAGLE

BASIN

RIVER MERSEY

Plan of Steel's shipyard, Queen's Dock, Liverpool. The boundaries are marked by heavy dotted lines. The other two dotted areas mark the tidal basins, which were filled in about 1852–3.

There was a building with a tall chimney that could have been the engine house of a sawmill. A plan prepared by the dock engineer of the Mersey Docks and Harbour Board in about 1880 shows extended buildings in the same positions as the earlier ones.[7] The northern ones were labelled smithy and mould room, the southern ones workshop and shipwright's shop. It is possible that these buildings had similar functions to the earlier Steel buildings and indeed probably incorporated them. There is one rather indistinct photograph of them, and a watercolour of a steamer on the stocks of Royden's yard next-door which shows the former Steel yard with substantial brick, slate-roofed buildings.[8] The best illustration of a well-established 'modern' shipyard of the second quarter of the 19th century is the detailed model of the Leith Shipyard of 1830 in the collection of the National Museum of Scotland. This has a similar long narrow space with workshops, including a sawmill, on either side of the central slipway.[9]

The map and pictorial evidence, poor though they are, suggest that Steel had a modern yard with brick buildings and a steam engine rather than the set of temporary sheds that so many other contemporary shipbuilders made do with. The yard was well placed to carry out repairs and fitting out because it was near to the two graving docks and the masting crane at Queen's half-tide dock and the grid-iron at King's Dock river wall. It also had good access to imported timber supplies, which were unloaded at Queen's Dock.[10] The small buildings fronting Baffin Street were probably offices and as Steel had no other commercial address in its shipyard days it was also the administrative centre for its merchanting and shipowning businesses. No trace of the yard or its buildings remains. W.H. Potter & Co built their last ship in 1899 and the site along with the Royden yard and the Eagle basin was incorporated in the modernisation of Queen's and King's Docks completed in 1905–6. Today it lies under Queen's Branch Dock no.1.[11]

Although other builders complained about the lack of space at their yards to the Liverpool Shipbuilding Committee, which had been set up to investigate the decline of this local industry in 1850, Joseph Steel junior gave evidence to it in which he expressed general satisfaction with his accommodation and access to the public graving docks. He thought that the proposed moving of the shipyards to the north docks would not be an improvement because of the exposure to gales from the north-west. He was, however, dissatisfied with his rent of £350 a year. He did not have a lease until 1852 (possibly), and short-term tenancies were considered a major problem since they impeded investment in buildings and machinery.[12] Steel also complained of lack of space for timber storage. Comparison with shipyards in other ports at the same period suggests that because of competition for scarce waterfront space many of them were even more confined. Builders of wooden ships needed large areas of open ground to sort and store timber. Photographs of yards in Sunderland, the major British competitor of the Liverpool shipbuilders, show a greater density of use than at Liverpool and yet these yards were capable of building ships larger than the *Jhelum*.[13]

The *Lloyd's Survey* of the *Jhelum* and those of two other ships, the *Zillah* (1847) and the *Helen Wallace* (1848), show that Steel was using the best possible materials in its ships. The major woods used included English oak and imported timbers such as 'African oak' and 'mahogany', ironwood and greenheart.[14] Liverpool was a major centre for imported timber especially that from Canada which had its own dedicated berth, Brunswick dock (1849), and tropical hardwoods from West Africa, the West Indies and South America. English oak was available in large quantities shipped coast-wise and along the canals from Shropshire and Wales. Liverpool was not an ironmaking centre, but 'the greatest shipping port for iron in the world.'[15] Large stocks were held in the town for both export and local use. Pig-iron consumption in 1853 was 58,000 tons, some of which would have been cast as ship's fittings, for example hawse ports, windlass and winch gears as on the *Jhelum*. Wrought iron was also in demand and 'the shipbuilders, anchor smiths, chain-cable makers, boiler makers, machine makers, nailmakers, blacksmiths, wheelwrights, etc consumed 15,000 tons of wrought iron last year. The whole of these trades are in a flourishing condition.'[16] While castings, anchors and chain cable would have been produced by specialist manufacturers, the wrought iron knees, including the Fell's patent version fitted to the *Jhelum*, the *Zillah* and the *Helen Wallace*, were probably made in the yard's own smithy. Copper bolts and sheathing plates made from yellow metal such as Muntz metal were stocked in Liverpool in large quantities for export, repair and new buildings. Copper was smelted and rolled inland at St Helens, which had good rail and water links with Liverpool. Cordage for rigging was locally made but canvas, which had earlier been a speciality of the nearby inland town of Warrington, came chiefly from Scottish textile centres such as Dundee.[17]

It is not known how many workers Steel employed to build its ships. In any case, the trade employed casual workers on daily wages and numbers would have fluctuated according to demand. An informed guess, based on Stewart-Brown's 18th-century figures and the workforces of other wooden shipyards elsewhere, suggests a figure of between thirty and sixty. The main body of craftsmen, the shipwrights, would have been directed to the building of the hull. They would have served a seven-year apprenticeship. Many apprentices were also employed as they were a source of cheap labour as well as of future craftsmen. A sub-group in Liverpool known as ship carpenters were less highly trained and worked less on manufacturing ships than on repairing them.[18] There were also sparmakers, who made masts and yards and could either be specialists or shipwrights and, similarly, there were specialist makers of treenails, blockmakers, sail-makers, caulkers and carvers of ship decorations. All or some of this work could be carried out 'in-house' or sub-contracted to specialist workshops. *Gore's Liverpool Directory* lists sail-making and block-making (often with pump-making) as separate activities in separate premises.

According to the Shipbuilding Committee minutes the total shipbuilding workforce in 1850 totalled 1,600 of whom between 850 and 1,200 were regularly unemployed, such was the decline in the local industry. It was also alleged that high wage rates had put up costs so much that shipowners were deterred from using Liverpool for repairs. The public graving docks could be rented by all and as they were mainly at a distance from the shipyards the masters had difficulty controlling the men and obtaining a fair day's work from them. The root cause of all the problems was considered to be 'the combination of carpenters'.[19] This had been formed in the 18th century and in 1784 it was referred to as The Liverpool Society of Shipwrights or the True British Society – All Freemen.[20] It regulated recruitment by maintaining the customary system of apprenticeships and all its members were freemen of the town and therefore entitled to vote at parliamentary elections. As a result it not only exercised power to negotiate over wages with the master shipbuilders but was also political. This meant that before the Reform Act of 1832 it negotiated the sale of its members' votes with rival candidates.[21] Parliamentary candidates still took the trouble to canvass the shipwrights after 1832. In 1835, the two contestants attended the launch of the *Mary Somerville* at Steel's yard to lobby the shipwrights:

> Launch of the *Mary Somerville* – yesterday at 11 o'clock the fine ship *Mary Somerville* built by Messrs. Steel and Company was launched from the yard of the builders in Baffin Street, Queens Dock. It having been announced that the two parliamentary candidates for the Borough, Lord Sandon and Sir Howard Douglas would be present to witness the gratifying marine ceremony, a great number of electors congregating anticipating that the candidates would take the opportunity of addressing the shipwrights. Lord Sandon then came forward and after stating that he did not think there could be a better opportunity for a candidate to address his constituents connected with maritime affairs than the present, especially after the noble sight they had witnessed, made an eloquent speech expressive of his determination to support the commerce of the County . . . Sir Howard Douglas proceeded to compliment the shipwrights on the beautiful specimen of British industry that had just been launched in which not only they, but the mercantile and maritime interests were so deeply interested. He was a staunch advocate of the shipping interest which was well known to them, as in consequence of his being first introduced into the electors of Liverpool.[22]

The shipwrights' society took strike action to enforce its power occasionally, levied subscriptions and built almshouses for its older members.[23] The current wage rate was five shillings a day and at the Shipbuilding Committee it was suggested that it would be an advantage to both men and masters if in return for guaranteed regular work it were reduced to four shillings.[24]

Whatever the difficulties of the relationship between shipwrights and employers, there is no doubt about the high standard of workmanship of Steel's ships. The *Jhelum* is evidence in herself, as the many small extra features such as mouldings on deck beams make clear. The three surviving reports of Lloyd's Surveyors all noted that the general quality of workmanship was either good or very good. Steel's ships, when classified, generally achieved between ten and thirteen years at A1. The lowest rated was the *Grand Bonny*, at seven years. It is not clear whether the Steels were master shipwrights who designed and supervised the building of their ships or managers employing a master shipwright as yard foreman. Our own guess would be the former because this was the case for most small shipyards at the time and their prudent approach to shipowning suggests the caution of newcomers to that business. Their shipbuilding business, however, was relatively innovative, making use of machinery for sawing timber, ironwork such as the Fell's patent knees, and the installation of iron water tanks.

The hull design of the *Jhelum* was typical of her date. Her registered dimensions were length 118.5 feet, breadth 24.6 feet and depth of hold 17 feet in her first registration. When she was re-registered under the new measurement rules in 1856, she measured 123.1 feet length, 27.1 feet breadth and 18.1 feet depth of hold, 428.35

gross tons. The latter set of dimensions is more useful because it enables the coeffi-
cient of under-deck tonnage to be calculated. This is a useful comparison and an
indication of fineness, together with the ratio of length to breadth. A sharp, fine-
lined vessel such as the clipper *Cutty Sark* is .55, while a bluff vessel is between .70
and .80. The *Jhelum* was of broadly similar proportions to her two immediate predecessors, the *Zillah* (342.08 tons) and the *Helen Wallace* (572.29 tons), and to a sample
of ships built in 1849 as shown in Table 2.1.

Table 2.1 Comparative dimensions of selected ships

	under-deck coefficient	length to breadth ratio
Jhelum	.70	4.56
Helen Wallace	.68	4.29
Zillah	.79	4.70
Sample of 50 ships built in 1849	.73	4.20

Ship design evolved fairly slowly between 1800 and 1850. There was a gradual
increase in tonnage and in length, and there were important innovations such as
the increased use of iron components, especially knees and stanchions. British
shipbuilders were protected by the Navigation Acts from foreign competitors.
They were also circumscribed by tonnage rules for registry, which tended to
favour deep bluff vessels, and by the rules of *Lloyd's Register* for classification. The
Jhelum was no clipper nor was she some obsolete aberration. Rather she was the
well-built latest edition of a well-proven design. Speed was only valuable if there
was a premium to be earned for fast passage. This only applied to packet trades

A wooden sailing ship under construction at Brocklebank's shipyard about 1859–65. She appears to be
about the same size as the *Jhelum* and may have been the ship *Juanpore* of 1859, 144.4 feet long and 459
tons. Steel's yard would have had a similar appearance.

such as the regular services to America or Australia. Breaking records made for good publicity and that attracted customers, and certain specialised freights such as tea, opium and fruit demanded fast ships.

Perhaps there has been too much emphasis on the 'clippers', for they were only a tiny proportion of the merchant marine in the mid-19th century and their real heyday only lasted from about 1850 to 1870. The study of the *Jhelum* and similar bulk carriers is a useful corrective. It has been suggested that her design was in some way based on that of the East India Company's ships. Whether the reference is to the Company's own vessels or its 'extras' is not clear. The description seems to have been applied to her after she was hulked, and has more to do with her name than any hard evidence. Liverpool built only a few East Indiamen and none after 1804.[25] We would prefer to regard her as a lineal descendant of Liverpool's West Indiamen and Guineamen. Lindsay characterised this when describing the West Indiaman *Thetis* as 'a fair representation of the type of vessel which had long been employed by the enterprising merchants of Bristol and Liverpool in their trade to the West Indies. Unlike the vessels of the East India Company her capacity for cargo was considerably in excess of her registered tonnage and her complement of crew less than one half in proportion to her tonnage. Nor were these vessels inferior to them in speed or other seagoing qualities, though they too were greatly surpassed by those of a later period.'[26]

A report of a court case to recover possession of an unfinished vessel being built at Sunderland in the Liverpool paper *Gore's Liverpool Advertiser* for March 23rd 1833 lends further weight to the idea of a Liverpool tradition of design. It recorded that the ship, which was being built for Liverpool owners, was designed by Mr Thomas Bland, shipbuilder of Bland and Chaloner of 5 Baffin Street. 'The vessel was to be built on the *Liverpool plan* and Mr Thomas Bland, shipbuilder went over to Sunderland, laid down the plans and furnished models, superintended the work for some time and during his absence left another person as his substitute.' It is interesting to note that Bland used both plans and a half model to specify the hull design. Steel doubtless followed the same practice with its ships.

In 1849, in addition to Steel there were 54 other firms listed in *Gore's Liverpool Directory* as shipbuilders. Ten were boat or canal barge builders. Sixteen had facilities to launch new vessels and the rest were ship repairers. Hodgson & Co at Brunswick Dock built iron ships and there was also the iron shipyard of Laird at Birkenhead. Laird and ten other yards launched no ships in 1849. The remaining six built five ocean-going sailing cargo ships, a pilot cutter and six paddle steamers (Table 2.2).

Table 2.2 Vessels completed at Liverpool in 1849

Builder	Vessel	Tons	Owner
Royden	*Lancastrian*	591	Tapley & Co, Liverpool
Royden	*Auspicious*	49	Liverpool Pilots
Chaloner	*Ranee*	590	I.H. Macintyre & Co, Liverpool
Steel	*Jhelum*	428	J. Steel & Co, Liverpool
Cato & Miller	*Badkham*	190	Lamport & Holt, Liverpool
Cato & Miller	*Cato*	127	Birkenhead Commissioners
	(iron paddle steam ferry)		

Vernon	*Fairy* (iron paddle steam ferry)	165	T. Coulburn, New Brighton
Vernon	*Sylph* (iron paddle steam ferry)	112.8	J. Crippin, Runcorn
Greenstreet & Paton	*Menai* (iron paddle steam ferry)	?	Menai Steam Packet Co
Liverpool Dock Trust★	*Earl of St Vincent*	107	For their use
Liverpool Steam Tug Co★	*Tartar*	241	For their own use

★These yards were engaged in ship repair rather than regular shipbuilding.
Sources: Liverpool (Statutory) Register of Ships 1849; Papers of A.C. Wardle, Liverpool Nautical Research Society Archive, Merseyside Maritime Museum; L. Lloyd, *The Port of Caernarfon 1793–1900* (Caernarfon, 1989), pp. 239–43 for information on the *Menai*.

The total tonnage of these twelve ships was about 3,300 tons compared with the 6,178 tons of the 22 ships built in 1835. Also in 1849, the biggest Canadian shipbuilding centre, St John, New Brunswick, built 22 ships, totalling 15,144 tons, and thirteen of those were sold to Liverpool owners.[27] In 1850 Sunderland launched 158 ships of a total 50,374 tons.[28] British shipbuilding production took a general downturn in 1848–9 after a peak in 1840–1.[29]

It is perhaps not surprising then that the Corporation of Liverpool, which owned the docks and the shipyards, reacted favourably to a petition of the shipbuilders which asked that a committee be set up to establish the causes of the local decline and suggest remedies. The causes have been covered earlier but in summary. They amounted to lack of space, lack of secure tenure, no private graving docks and high wage costs. The Committee did try to address the problems and made a recommendation that the Queen's Dock shipyards' accommodation should be improved by building a proper river wall, filling in the two inlets, rationalising the boundaries and granting fourteen-year leases with a cancellation clause after seven years. The wall improvement and the filling-in were certainly carried out, at a cost of about £6,500, and the leases were probably granted.[30] While this did improve the site, it was tinkering with a problem that was probably insuperable in the short term. The products of Canadian competitors, which accounted for more than 50 per cent of Liverpool-registered ships, were cheaper although there is debate as to what the difference was. G.F. Young, a Liverpool shipowner of the 1840s and Chairman of the General Shipowner's Society, reckoned it to be as much as £3 to £4 a ton. Sagar believes this is an exaggeration because of costly inputs other than cheap timber and labour – ironwork, for example – which eroded the difference to about 15 shillings to £1 per ton or 10 per cent of the selling price. A typical 300-ton Canadian vessel might sell for £3,000 (£10 per ton) and earn another £600 on a freight of timber on the delivery voyage to Liverpool.[31] The Canadians enjoyed a semi-closed market in the United Kingdom, only competing with native builders until the Navigation Acts were repealed in 1849; even after that Canadian ships were sold in greater quantity than those of the other main competitor, the USA.[32] On the other hand, Canadian vessels were considered to be of poor quality, both in workmanship and materials, although there has been debate as to whether this opinion was British prejudice and as to what the precise strengths of North American woods such as hackmatack, white oak and pitch pine were. Sagar quotes H.C. Chapman, a Liverpool shipowner: 'I did not know which was the most dangerous thing a colonial ship or a race horse', but also notes a gradual improvement in quality because of greater supervision by Lloyd's Surveyors and a greater readiness to use better-quality materials, such as live oak which had to be imported from the Southern states. Even so, the highest classification that Canadian ships were awarded was seven years but the average price range was £4–7 per ton. A Sunderland 7A1 years ship cost between £10 and £12 per ton.[33] In 1850, a Liverpool built ship cost much more. W. Fisher, one of the builders questioned by the Shipbuilding Committee, stated that an accurate cost for a 500-ton ship rated at A1 for ten to twelve years was between £8,800 and £10,800, or between £17 12s and £21 12s a ton. This was broken down into costs of £3,000 to £4,000 for timber, the same for labour, £900 for sails and ropes, £500 for metal work, £400 for coppering, £500 for chandlery (including paint) and £500 for furniture.[34]

The *Joseph Steel*, which was completed in 1854, was valued on the death of Joseph Steel senior at £6,996 for 24 shares, which gives £20.72 per ton.[35] The *Jhelum* probably cost about the same and the reason why Steel invested in expensive vessels will be examined in the next chapter. Joseph Steel junior continued the business after his father's death and did not go bankrupt, as has been stated in the Wardle Papers and repeated in later articles. The bankrupt they cite was in fact a James Steel, a timber merchant of a different address who may or may not have been related to the ship-builders.[36] Joseph gave up shipbuilding to concentrate on shipowning and merchanting in 1859. Some of his colleagues in the Master Shipbuilders' Society survived and flourished, but not by trying to compete in wooden shipbuilding. Iron was the up-and-coming material. In 1850, out of a total United Kingdom tonnage of 133,695 tons launched, only 12,800 was iron. By 1860 out of a total of 211,968 tons, 147,629 was wood and 64,699 was iron, and by 1868 out of 369,573 tons 208,101 was iron and 161,472 tons was wood.[37] The Liverpool and Mersey shipbuilding industry had revived by 1854, producing at least 5,110 tons at Liverpool (mainly four large iron sailing vessels) and another 10,115 tons of iron steamers at Lairds, Birkenhead.[38] And what did Steel's buy after 1863? – iron ships!

Notes

1. *Gore's Liverpool Advertiser*, 7th June 1849.
2. Communication from Anthony Steel, present owner of the family estate, Kirkwood near Lockerbie, Scotland.
3. A. Wardle, notebook on Liverpool shipbuilders, Liverpool Nautical Research Society Collection, Merseyside Maritime Museum.
4. Joseph Steel junior's evidence to the Special Committee appointed by the Liverpool Town Council to consider the state of shipbuilding in Liverpool in 1850 (subsequently referred to as the Shipbuilding Committee Evidence, L.N.R.S. Collection, M.M.M.). See also Liverpool Corporation Records, Shipbuilding Committee Minutes, 352 MIN SH1/1, Liverpool Record Office.
5. A.R. Burstall, *Shipbuilding in Liverpool* (Liverpool, 1935).

6.   J. Masefield, *The Wanderer of Liverpool* (London, 1930), p. 1.

7.   Mersey Docks and Harbour Board Collection, M.M.M.

8.   N.R. Ritchie-Noakes, *Liverpool's Historic Waterfront* (London, 1984), plate 27, and M.M.M. Collection, accession number 84–466.

9.   National Museum of Scotland, accession no. 1949.11.

10. Ritchie-Noakes, *Liverpool's Historic Waterfront*, p. 40.

11. M.D.H.B. Collection, M.M.M.

12. Shipbuilding Committee Evidence and Minutes, see note 4.

13. D.R. MacGregor, *Fast Sailing Ships* (London, 1988), p. 138.

14. *Lloyd's Register Surveys* nos. 17615, 18262, 18405, National Maritime Museum, Greenwich. Samples of the 'African oak' on the *Jhelum* were identified as *Khaya* sp. and orere by Angus Gunn of the Botany Department, Liverpool Museum.

15. B. Poole, *The Commerce of Liverpool* (Liverpool, 1854), Vol. 1, p. 47.

16. *Ibid.*, p. 51.

17. *Ibid.* lists many of these materials and *Gore's Liverpool Directory* indicates which were manufactured in the town.

18. R. Stewart-Brown, *Liverpool Ships in the 18th Century* (Liverpool, 1932), p. 34. Shipbuilding Committee Minutes, 19th September 1850, p. 34 noting the disadvantages of public graving docks; they 'had the effect of bringing up an inferior class of carpenters brought up to mere repairing and not thorough masters of the business of a Shipwright'.

19. Shipbuilding Committee Minutes, as note 18.

20. Stewart-Brown, *Liverpool Ships*, p. 40.

21. S.& B. Webb, *The History of Trade Unionism* (1920), pp. 39–40.

22. *Gore's Liverpool Advertiser*, 1st January 1835.

23. Stewart-Brown, *Liverpool Ships*, p. 41, and there is a model of the alms-houses, a membership card and a celebratory jug in the M.M.M. collections.

24. Shipbuilding Committee Minutes, as note 18.

25. M. Bound, 'The Hulk *Jhelum* a Derivative Expression of Late British Indiaman Building', *International Journal of Nautical Archaeology and Underwater Exploration*, xix (1), pp. 43–7.

26. W.S. Lindsay, *History of Merchant Shipping and Ancient Commerce* (London, 1874), Vol. 2, pp. 490–1.

27. F. Neal, 'Liverpool Shipping in the Early 19th Century', in *Liverpool and Merseyside*, ed. J.R. Harris (1969), p. 170, table XIV; E.C. Wright, *St. John Ships and Their Builders* (Wolfville, Canada, 1976), pp. 181–2, 184–5.

28. J.W. Smith and T.S. Holden, *Where Ships are Born, Sunderland 1346–1946* (Sunderland, 1949), originally in the *Nautical Magazine*, XXI (1852), p. 593.

29. E.W. Sagar with G. Panting *Maritime Capital*, (Montreal, 1990), p. 33.

30. Shipbuilding Committee Minutes, 5th October 1852, p. 62. The fourteen-year leases had a precedent in the lease granted to Hodgson & Co iron shipbuilders at the less developed site at Brunswick Dock in 1845. Alsop Wilkinson Collection, M.M.M.

31. Sagar with Panting, *Maritime Capital*, p. 36.

32. M.K. Stammers, 'The Jhelum and the Liverpool Shipbuilders', in *Liverpool Shipping, Trade and Industry*, ed. V. Burton (Liverpool, 1989), p. 84, table 3.

33. Sagar with Panting, *Maritime Capital*, p. 36.

34. Shipbuilding Committee Evidence, L.N.R.S. Collection, M.M.M.

35. Steel Family Archives, cf Alexander Stephen & Sons, quoting £17–20 per ton in 1855 in D.R. MacGregor, *Fast Sailing Ships*, p. 136.

36. *Liverpool Chronicle*, 20th November 1858.

37. Figures quoted by John Laird, MP, in *The Practical Magazine*, 1874.

38. Cammell Laird list of vessels, Wardle Papers, L.N.R.S. Collection, M.M.M.

CHAPTER THREE

MANAGING THE
JHELUM

Joseph Steel built the *Enterprise* on his own account in 1835, probably with the original intention of keeping key members of his workforce employed. She was probably laid down speculatively in the hope that a buyer would be found. When this did not happen, he used her for trading himself. This was not uncommon: Alexander Stephen at Dundee built the *Asia* in 1847 and traded with her until he was able to sell her for £5,000 in 1850.[1] However, once Joseph Steel had operated one vessel he began to build a small fleet. Shipbuilder-shipowners were not uncommon. Fell of Warrington, Deslandes of Jersey, Brocklebank of Whitehaven, Green of London, the Hill family of Bristol and Royden of Liverpool were examples. Brocklebank started building at Whitehaven in 1789 and by 1850 was building ships almost exclusively for its own fleet. Brocklebank was also a merchant firm, as was Joseph Steel. Steel's first shipowning venture must have been a success because he and his son built more vessels on their own account after 1839. By 1843, they owned five vessels:

- The brig *Birkby* (323 tons) built at Workington in 1825, trading to Montreal
- The ship *Enterprise* (338 tons), their own building in 1836, Liverpool to Calcutta
- The barque *Buenos Ayrean* (349 tons), their own building in 1840, Liverpool to Calcutta
- The ship *Livingstone* (407 tons), their own building in 1840, Liverpool to Calcutta
- The ship *Dorisana* (486 tons), their own building in 1843, Liverpool to Calcutta

The *Enterprise* was classified for nine years at A1 and the three other ships built by Steel were classified for twelve years on the *Liverpool Register*, which was set up in 1835 to provide more accurate assessments of local ships than those provided by *Lloyd's Register* in London.[2] The *Birkby*, an older vessel, was voyaging between Liverpool and Montreal possibly hauling timber, the usual trade for older ships sailing to Canada. The new ships were all in the Calcutta trade and were of similar size to other Liverpool vessels listed as sailing to India.

Because of Liverpool's rapid growth there was no shortage of cargo for its ships. Although there were cycles of booms and depressions, trading volume grew rapidly in the first half of the 19th century. By 1850, 3,536,300 tons of shipping entered the port, compared with 450,100 tons in 1800. Liverpool became the nation's leading

The portrait of the Liverpool ship *Helen* of 1840 is similar to the *Jhelum*'s appearance as a full-rigged ship.

export port and shipped out £34,891,847 of goods in 1850, compared with £14,137,527 at London and £10,366,610 at Hull. London led Liverpool in imports, with goods valued at £43,138,821, compared with £37,404,400.[3] Liverpool's most important exports were cotton and woollen cloth, salt, glass, soap, cutlery, pottery, machinery, hardware and part-finished iron, copper, lead and tinplate; the leading imports were cotton (valued at £15,000,000 – five-sixths of United Kingdom imports), grain, flour, sugar, tobacco, wool, metal ores, hemp and timber.[4] The locally owned fleet expanded rapidly to meet demand. In 1835 there were 207,093 tons on the local register and by 1854 this had risen to 687,220 tons, plus coasting vessels of under 100 tons.[5]

The biggest trade, to the USA, was dominated by American-owned vessels, but there were opportunities elsewhere. The Indian trade, which had been freed from the East India Company's monopoly in 1813, had grown rapidly between 1830 and 1840, chiefly because of the booming demand for raw cotton. Liverpool's Indian cotton imports increased from 12,276 bales in 1830 to 54,560 in 1835 and doubled again in 1836, the year Steel's *Enterprise* was finished.[6] It was perhaps not surprising that once

Steel & Co. had decided to build on its own account it traded to the East. After the success of its first venture it built up a fleet and after 1844 all but two of its ships were built on its own account. However, the company took a prudent approach to shipowning; it did not mortgage its vessels, nor expand the fleet beyond about ten ships. It also shared ownership – Steel had 32 shares in the *Jhelum* with 16 held by her captain, William Bell, and a further 16 held by Joseph Witham Coull, who had been the captain of the *Buenos Ayrean* in 1843. It was common practice to sell shares to the master, thus stimulating him to manage the vessel as well as he could. If he was fortunate, he could build up enough capital to become a shipowner in his own right.

Steel & Co. may well have ploughed much of the profits from the ship's freights back into the yard to build further ships. There could have been a cycle of investment from 1844 to 1859 that enabled the company to keep the shipyard going, despite competition. Perhaps it hoped that eventually the market would pick up and that further outside orders would come in. In 1859, when the lease was due for renewal, Joseph Steel junior must have decided that there was no future in wooden shipbuilding and was not prepared to invest in iron, unlike his neighbours the Roydens, and chose to be solely a shipowner. This was of course the way that many family businesses had to operate in the 19th century when trading risks were high. They had to take opportunities to diversify or move on as required. The Steels moved on from shipbuilding to shipowning and merchanting, and eventually became owners of a country estate in Scotland. When sailing ships began to look increasingly unprofitable, the company gradually sold all its vessels in the early 1900s. Steel & Co. had a choice of finding additional capital to buy steamers or finding other uses for its capital. In its case, it turned to merchant banking. Another firm, Royden, ran its shipyard until 1893 in tandem with shipowning, including a successful steamship company from 1880. The 20th-century descendants of the original Thomas Royden became directors in the Cunard Steamship Company. The capital invested by Steel & Co. in shipowning was never great compared with the big shipowners in Liverpool. But it did increase between 1854 and 1881. In 1854, on Joseph Steel senior's death, his five wholly owned ships were worth £25,005; in 1881, Joseph Steel junior died, leaving eight ships worth £47,105.[7]

The *Jhelum*, like her predecessors was no doubt intended for the India trade. Indeed, the name came from a tributary of the River Indus that had been the scene of an engagement between Indian and British forces in 1848. She was probably loaded with a 'general cargo'. The Liverpool Customs Bills of Entry were published daily and recorded the foreign imports and exports of the port, coastal traffic and ships entered for loading and cleared outwards by the customs authorities.[8] They also gave details of the master, the number of crew, the dock, the agents and the names of the consignees of the cargo (except where 'order' or 'to order' is inserted). They do not, however, assign exports to particular ships but to the destination port. With several ships entered for loading at Bombay at the same time as the *Jhelum* it is impossible to tell what she loaded. She would have carried a maximum of between 600 and 700 tons and a 'general cargo' was usually made up of iron bars and metal goods for ballast topped off with foodstuffs, wines, spirits and textiles. Baines noted that Liverpool was 'the outlet for the iron of Staffordshire, Yorkshire and North Wales; and, from the lowness of Liverpool freights for conveying metals, it is a great place of export for

Joseph Steel junior, shipbuilder and shipowner.

iron, copper, lead, tin and tinned plates. Iron, especially, being very useful for ballast is carried to the most distant parts of the world at very trifling expense, in vessels ladened with cottons, woollens, linens and silks, which has been shown, are found in greater abundance at Liverpool than at any other port of the empire.'[9]

The *Jhelum* was entered for loading at Salthouse dock from 1st June 1849 and cleared for Bombay on 12th July.[10] She reached Bombay on 16th November, a passage of 127 days for 6,255 miles and returned to Liverpool in 100 days. According to David MacGregor these were respectable passages for a ship of her size. The record for the outward passage (though from London, an extra 41 miles) was made by the 1,745 ton *Tweed* in 77 days in 1863. The *Parkfield* made the home passage from Bombay to Liverpool in 1836 in 75 days.[11]

The *Jhelum*'s cargo on her return voyage consisted of 2,190 bales and 70 half bales of cotton, 352 bags of myrobolams, 1,100 bags of coir, 500 bags of linseed, 2¹/₂ tons of deer horns, a box of boots and 5 bundles of carpets. It is likely that she shipped about 40 or 50 tons of blue granite ballast in the bottom of the hold with dunnage wood on top and split bamboo along the sides of the hold to protect the cargo. Bombay bales were pressed to contain 400 pounds of cotton, forming an oblong 51 by 24 by 18 inches. Four were reckoned to make a ton at a rate of 50 cubic feet of hold space.[12] This would make the *Jhelum*'s cotton cargo (2,225 whole bales) 556 tons.

Myrobolams or mirabolines are the dried fruit of a tree of the *terminalia* species, look rather like acorns, and were used in tanning leather. About 14 bags made up a ton, so the total cargo was about 25 tons.[13] Coir is a yarn made from the hairy outer husk of coconuts, and linseed, which was crushed for its oil for use in paints etc., was a major Indian export. It was usually stowed in the tween decks. It measured 14 bags to the ton, which made 78½ tons on the *Jhelum*.[14] Deer horn made good knife handles. The total cargo would have amounted to 662 tons, plus 50–60 tons of ballast and the coir, whose weight is unknown. This was a full cargo. It is not known what it earned the Steels, but Stevens refers to a Liverpool ship earning £2 5s a ton for Indian cotton in 1861.[15] The *Jhelum*'s cotton freight would thus have been worth £1,248 at that rate. Although some of these commodities may seem rather bizarre, all were regular items in the Indian–Liverpool trade. Total Liverpool imports in 1850 for the goods carried on the *Jhelum* were as follows: myrobolams, 17,516 cwt; linseed, 44,909 cwt; coir, 31,698 cwt; and deer horns, 2,778 cwt.[16]

The *Jhelum* arrived at Albert Dock on 17th April 1850, a 100-day passage. In these times of container ships it is easy to forget what a lengthy business foreign commerce was in the sailing ship era. The *Jhelum*'s performance was neither good nor bad but average, and for the rest of her career she performed about one round voyage every nine to twelve months. Loading and discharging was often at anchor using small barges in open roadsteads. This was especially true on the west coast of South America, and bad weather, shipping congestion and shortages of barges could seriously delay work. At Liverpool and other European ports of call ships came alongside quays where there was great pressure on space and cargoes were therefore discharged more quickly. Loading general cargo took longer because it was usually in small consignments.

The Albert Dock had been opened in 1846 and was designed to speed up the handling of valuable foreign imports, especially cotton. It had hydraulic cranes to discharge instead of the ships making use of their own handwinches with a gin-block suspended over the hatch and it had covered quays for sorting, weighing, recording and marking the cargo. Its upper floors and the vaults below could be used to store goods in bond. According to the Liverpool Customs Bill of Entry it took a week to discharge the *Jhelum*'s cargo. It is impossible to estimate what Steel earned on the round voyage. Assuming a full cargo outwards and certainly a full one home it could have been considerable. But the costs could also be considerable, including crew wages for about seven months, insurance for the ship, repairs and replacements of equipment (probably negligible on a maiden voyage, and the *Jhelum* arrived at Bombay well away from the monsoon season), pilotage, light and port dues, costs of loading and discharging, provisions and supplies for the voyage, drydocking before the next voyage, and commission to agents, brokers and the master.

The best parallel seems to be the running costs of the Falkland Island Company's ship the *Vicar of Bray*, which was of similar size, date and build to the *Jhelum*. She cost £1,450 a year to run in 1876 and was capable of earning about £1000 per round voyage. The accounts for the *Warlock*, a Liverpool-owned barque of 290 tons help to illuminate the details of the running costs. In 1853, for example they included £7 for towage from dock to sea, £4 1s for refitting the medicine chest, 5s for repairing four compasses, 7s 6d for cartage of the mizzen to the ship, £13 17s 6d for three barrels of Irish port, and 5s 6d for water supplied at Albert Dock.[17]

Although the *Jhelum* was entered for loading again at the Customs House on 25th April, it is likely that she went into one of the two Canning graving docks for scraping

down, caulking and painting before being moved into Salthouse Dock to load her
export cargo. Canning Dock and Salthouse Dock lay next to Albert Dock and so ships
emptied of their imports could be moved to load up for outward despatch in
Salthouse or to one of Canning's graving docks for routine maintenance. In dock with
her crew paid off, the *Jhelum* would have been shifted by 'riggers' who used the quayside bollards and capstans and the warping buoys in the centre of each dock to move
her.

In April 1850, Steel embarked on an experiment. The company's ships had mainly
traded with India, but for the *Jhelum*'s second voyage it was decided to send her to the
west coast of South America – to Arica on the northern frontier of Chile. The company decided to send its newest ship because this was a more difficult passage than the
one to India, covering 6,617 miles with two transits of Cape Horn. What determined
the change is unclear; trade to Chile and Peru could be difficult because of high insurance rates (6–12 per cent) on cargo, lack of demand for English goods because of the
high prices charged, the difficulties of communication and the need for long-term
credit.[18] This was especially so for a small port like Arica; perhaps the Liverpool
brokers W. & J. Tyrer and Ashley Brothers had enough freight offered to warrant the
Jhelum being despatched there. She could certainly pick up a good return cargo of
nitrates, copper or wool. In the event, the voyage was a success and she continued to
trade to the west coast until Steel sold her in 1863.

Whatever the difficulties there was a general perception that trade opportunities
existed in Chile and Peru. These countries offered new markets for British goods and
could supply important raw materials. The main ones included copper, wool, nitrate
of soda and guano. The last two were valuable fertilizers, and in demand because
Britain still depended chiefly on its own farmers to feed its growing urban population.
Nitrate of soda, 'Chile saltpetre' or nitrates were dug from the dry desert coasts of
northern Chile and Peru and shipped from ports such as Arica, Islay, Iquique and
Mexillones from about 1830. These were all anchorage ports where the cargo was
lightered out to the ship. Nitrate cargoes had to be carefully carried in sound vessels
because they could give off dangerous gas if wetted.[19]

Guano was bird droppings from the offshore islands of Peru. Huge flocks of seabirds
feeding off the rich fish stocks had created mountains of guano in these rainless
regions. The local inhabitants had long known about its fertilizing properties, and it
had been reserved for their own use. About 1838–9, the Peruvian government
decided to test the European market. A pilot shipment of 30 bags of South American
guano was landed at Liverpool on July 23rd 1839. The first full cargo of 327 tons
arrived (also at Liverpool) on the *Charles Eyes* from Valparaiso.[20] It was a success and
agricultural writers praised its value. The 'Old Norfolk Farmer' wrote in his *Agriculture
Ancient and Modern* about 1862: 'This now celebrated and favourite manure was, as we
have stated brought into Europe about 1840. It was sold, in the first instance at £20
per ton and was found to be so powerful as a manure, that it was said to pay even at
that high rate.' The Peruvian sort was considered the best and averaged around £10
per ton delivered to England.

Guano shipments were controlled through British agents appointed by the Peruvian
government and every vessel had to call at Callao, the port of the capital, Lima, to be
surveyed and if necessary repaired before being chartered and permitted to sail for the

Two three-masted barques of about the same tonnage as the *Jhelum* loading guano at the Chincha Islands in 1861. The one on the right carried a studding sail yard on the foremast, a try sail and a skysail on the mainmast. The guano was brought down from the huge hill-like deposits by mule-powered tramway and tipped into lighters.

Chincha Islands, the main source of guano, to load. Ships also had to call at Callao to clear customs before setting sail for England. Like nitrates, guano could be dangerous if wetted when it could give off ammonia fumes and affect the stability of the ship. It could also corrode ironwork in the hold, and rot sails and rigging.[21] Carriage of such cargoes could explain why the *Jhelum* was fitted with iron water tanks instead of wooden barrels.

Copper was mined inland and shipped in rough bars, or as grain copper, called 'barilla', in small canvas bags. Tin was shipped in the same manner. It was brought down from Tacua by llamas and from thence to Arica by railway. Like all dead-weight, such cargoes could strain the ship and make it too stiff. They had to be stowed as high as possible. 'In a ship of 420 tons register, an experienced master has always stowed them in the tween decks right fore and aft from bulkhead to bulkhead in tiers of six blocks abreast, occupying about 5 feet only in width. Deals fixed on their edges each side of the ship, right fore and aft, form a sort of baby trunk which is safely fastened to the tween deck stanchions. This plan not only relieves the wings, but secures the full support of the centre stanchions of the lower hold.'[22]

Thus copper (or tin) was also a difficult cargo that needed a strong vessel like the *Jhelum*. Wool from the alpaca was in great demand and generally shipped from Arica and Islay between November and January in bales weighing between 150 and 180 lbs and measuring 3 by 2 feet.[23] It complemented a deadweight cargo like nitrates or copper.

All the thirteen voyages the *Jhelum* made between 1850 and her sale in 1863 were to the west coast of South America: twelve to Chile or Peru and one to Guayaquil in Ecuador. All except voyage 9, which carried guano, involved either nitrates, copper or wool with small consignments of other commodities. All cargoes were delivered to Liverpool except for one to Baltimore and one to Hamburg but even after these two voyages the *Jhelum* returned to Liverpool to load general cargo outwards. Voyage 12 was the exception, when she loaded coal. Voyage 4, which was completed at the Albert Dock on Wednesday 19th October 1853, was an interesting example of the mixture with a cargo that consisted of 5,910 bags of copper or copper barilla, 1,290 bags of tin barilla, 65 bars of tin, 3,672 bags of nitrates, 1980 bags of wool, small consignments of hides, sheep and chinchilla skins, and two boxes of dollars.[24] This and voyages 6 and 9, together with evidence in *Gore's Liverpool Directory*, indicate that Steel & Sons were general merchants. In voyages 4 and 6 they did not own the bulk of the import cargo. They imported nitrates and smaller items; but on voyage 9 they had the whole consignment of 500 tons of guano.

It is impossible to tell how far they were involved in ownership of the outward export cargo. Apart from three occasions when the *Jhelum* sailed for Arica twice (voyages 2 and 4) and Guayaquil (voyage 11) once, she was entered for Valparaiso and it is impossible to disentangle her cargo from other ships also entered for that port. For example, in 1853–4 (probably June to June) thirty-three ships left for Valparaiso from Liverpool.[25] Voyage 2 is the best example of outward cargo. From 2nd May 1850, the *Jhelum* was the only vessel entered for Arica and from then until 6th June, two days before sailing, she received small consignments of textiles, hardware, stationery, earthenware, timber, beer, wine, chemicals, iron, musical instruments, 'corahs', glass, lace, jewellery, candles and 'smallware'. The textiles amounted to 256 bales, 130 trunks, 81 cases and 37 boxes and were mainly cottons and woollens. It is impossible to determine how many of each type there were because they were mixed; for example on 4th May 1850 there were 38 bales, 10 cases and 12 trunks of cotton and woollens loaded. The 32$\frac{1}{2}$ tons of bar iron, which was clearly the ballast, was loaded quite late on the 18th and 31st May. This cargo would not have filled the hold. The slowness of loading must have been a reflection both of the difficulty in finding a cargo and the use of a hand winch through the narrow hatches of a sailing ship. The *Jhelum* carried very similar goods on voyages 4 and 11.

Steel & Co. succeeded in employing the *Jhelum* from 1849 to 1863 when she needed a Lloyd's special survey. She had not in fact been classified by Lloyd's or the Liverpool Committee. But her construction was the equivalent of twelve years at A1. She seems to have sailed without major repairs on a difficult route with difficult and dangerous cargoes – a great testimony to her builders and her masters. Steel & Co., like any shipowner of this period, was very dependent on the good business sense of its masters and the appointment of trustworthy agents in South America who would organise freights, advance money to the master, and see to business matters such as the payment of dues for lights, harbour, hospitals and repairs. They would take a percentage commission (often $2^1/_2$ per cent) for their work.

There was only one reference to any damage to the *Jhelum* in *Lloyd's List*. The issue of 6th June 1854 reported a severe storm at Valparaiso on 6th May in which the *Jhelum* was 'severely damaged'. She did not leave there for Iquique until 27th July, which may indicate that repairs were carried out as well as unloading. Incidentally, the *Lloyd's List* report demonstrated the length of time information took to get back to England. Voyage times were quite creditable, the best being Liverpool to Valparaiso on voyage 5 in 96 days. The best return passage was on voyage 2, 93 days from Islay to Liverpool. The longest was voyage 11 Liverpool to Guayaquil and return, but Guayaquil was well to the north of the *Jhelum*'s usual calling places. Basil Lubbock, the great authority on passage times, especially record-breaking ones, recorded a number for vessels of about the size of the *Jhelum*. The barque *Margaret Gibson* of 540 tons, for example, made a fast trip of 86 days from Liverpool to Valparaiso in 1876. The barque *Lillian Morris* sailed from Talcahuano to Falmouth in 105 days sometime between 1877 and 1889.[26]

The *Jhelum* must have earned its owner sufficient to carry on as shipbuilders. Steel & Son built another six ships for its own use in the 1850s and in the year of her sale the company could afford to invest in an iron ship to continue its business – the *Eden*, a barque of 493 gross tons built by J. Pearce at Stockton-on-Tees in 1863. She was the first of Steel's iron ships, which gradually replaced its own wooden ships over the next ten years.[27]

Notes

1. D.R. MacGregor, *Merchant Sailing Ships 1815–50* (London, 1984), p. 100.
2. *Liverpool Commercial Register 1843* and M.K. Stammers, 'The Jhelum and the Liverpool Shipbuilders', in *Liverpool Shipping, Trade and Industry*, ed. V. Burton (Liverpool, 1989), p. 82.
3. F.E. Hyde, *Liverpool and the Mersey* (Newton Abbot, 1971), p. 237.
4. T. Baines, *History and Commerce of the Town of Liverpool* (London and Liverpool, 1852), pp. 744-5.
5. First figure from F. Neal, 'Liverpool Shipping in the Early 19th Century', in *Liverpool and Merseyside*, ed. J.R. Harris (1969), p. 157, table IV, and the second from Stammers, 'The Jhelum', p. 83.
6. Figures from D.M. Williams, 'Liverpool Merchants and the Cotton Trade 1820–50', in *Liverpool and Merseyside*, ed. J.R. Harris (London, 1969), p. 83.
7. Steel family archives.
8. Liverpool Record Office Collection.
9. Baines, *History and Commerce*, p. 761.
10. See Appendix 3 for sources of this date and all subsequent voyage dates.
11. *Lloyd's Calendar* (London, 1913), pp. 570–2, 578.
12. R.W. Stevens, *On the Stowage of Ships and their Cargoes* (London and Plymouth, 7th edn, 1893, first published 1858), p. 157. n.b., all the examples quoted date from the 1850s and 1860s and *Liverpool Customs Bill of Entry*.
13. Stevens, *On the Stowage of Ships*, pp. 426–7.
14. *Ibid.*, pp. 556–7.
15. *Ibid.*, p. 163.
16. T. Baines, *History and Commerce*, p. 785.
17. Falkland Islands Co. Archives, F. E. Cobb to Directors, London, 37, April 9th 1878 and Warlock Papers, Merseyside Maritime Museum.

18. D.M. Platt, *Latin America and British Trade 1806–1914* (London, 1972), p. 55.

19. Stevens, *On the Stowage of Ships*, pp. 538–45.

20. *Gore's Liverpool Directory Annals of Liverpool 1895* (reprinted Liverpool, 1981), and commemorated in painting by Joseph Heard, M.M.M.

21. Stevens, *On the Stowage of Ships*, pp. 291–9.

22. *Ibid.*, p. 151.

23. *Ibid.*, p. 796.

24. *Liverpool Customs Bill of Entry* no. 10670, October 19th 1853.

25. Mersey Docks & Harbour Board Collection Leg/A7/39, M.M.M.

26. B. Lubbock, *The Last of the Windjammers* (Glasgow, 1927), Vol. 1, pp. 394–6.

27. Steel's *Tinto* (1852), survived the longest and worked under sail in various ownerships up to about 1917 when some Germans sailed her to Germany from Chile. She became a salt storage hulk at Bergen, Norway, until about 1948 when she was scuttled.

CHAPTER FOUR

CAPTAINS AND CREWS

The Agreements and Accounts of the Crew and the *Official Log Books* demanded by the Board of Trade are prize sources of evidence for the captains and crews of the *Jhelum*. These documents have been divided between the Maritime History Group's archives at the Memorial University, Newfoundland, and the Public Record Office and National Maritime Museum in London. These three sources have yielded the names of 326 men who served aboard the *Jhelum*, on voyages 2 to 3, 7 to 15 and 17 to 19.

There are six known captains of the *Jhelum*. William Bell, who hailed from Newcastle, commanded her from 1849 to 1856; William Crawford of Elgin, Scotland, from 1856 to 1858; John Seymour of Bridport, Dorset, from 1858 to 1860; Archibald Garrioch from the Orkney Islands from 1860 to 1863; James Stannus from Carrickfergus, County Antrim, from 1863 to 1869; and J.L.G. Beaglehole of Dartmouth, Devon, from 1869 to 1871. It is likely that the *Jhelum* was the first command of Crawford, and possibly of Garrioch. Crawford, for example came from the *Oliver Lang*, which was one of the largest clippers of the Liverpool–Australian Black Ball Line and at 33 it is unlikely that he held a higher position than first mate of the vessel. Bell and Beaglehole were both 41 when they took over, and Seymour and Garrioch were 33 and 31. These latter two also had the advantage that they had come from other Steel-owned ships – the *Helen Wallace* and the *Toftcombs* – and Seymour had in fact worked for Steel since 1850.[1] Bell and Stannus served longest of the five. The others served either two or three voyages. Bell and Stannus both had shares in the vessel, which explains their longer tenure.

The master's responsibilities were wide-ranging and often laid down in a set of written instructions from his owner. One Liverpool example summarised them as 'maintaining good discipline on board, and pursuing the business of your vessel with energy and exercising careful economy in regard to her disbursements'.[2] Most of the specific instructions were concerned with avoiding expenses abroad, and ensuring that cargoes were surveyed, protests made, charter parties authenticated, bills of lading specified and bills of exchange drawn on reputable houses. These gave general guidance but the master might have to make decisions about his ship's business on the spot, especially if his owners were not represented by an agent in a particular port. Communications from the west coast of South America could take about two months. In 1857, for example, the *Jhelum* arrived on 2nd October but this information did not appear in *Lloyd's List* until 3rd December. Steel's would have had agents or 'correspondents' in the main ports of Valparaiso and Callao, and the *Jhelum* called there to deliver cargo and to collect orders. She might have secured a charter-party for the homeward voyage which would have been posted to meet the *Jhelum*'s arrival. The agents were of vital assistance because of their local knowledge, and were paid on a commission: 'Having arrived at the foreign port of loading', one contemporary master's manual put it, 'your duty is to put yourself under the charge of the agent for the shippers, or the ship, if there be one. To one or other of these you will have to entrust the clearing of the vessel, and doing what is necessary to permit her to load, of which it cannot be expected that you yourself can have a competent knowledge.'[3]

The master had wide powers over the crew: 'In regulating the hours of duty, sleep, meals, etc, the master has absolute power.'[4] He also had to be a judge of character when recruiting and there never seems to have been a shortage of men. As the contemporary master's manual put it:

> One of the first requisites of a seaman is his character. I do not mean his character as a mere sailor – for you often find the best sailor to be the greatest rogue and to be a person, on no account, you should have on board your ship. But by a seaman's character, I mean his moral character – a man who does his duty from principle, not because he is compelled to do it and on whose honesty and veracity you can place great dependence . . . Masters, ought when it can be done, to select their seamen as domestic servants on shore are selected. You do not admit a servant into your family until you have ascertained both that she is capable of performing the work she has undertaken, and that her moral character is unexceptionable.[5]

In fact, joining the ship in a drunken stupor, refusing orders and deserting were very common; and the master had powers under the Mercantile Marine Act of 1850 to deduct fines from the crew's wages, dismiss offenders or place them in irons. The minimum fine was half a day's pay and included apparently minor offences such as swearing on deck. Corporal punishment was not unknown but not of the formal kind like flogging in the Royal Navy. Oppressive treatment, the master's manual suggested, was usually counter-productive: 'Knowing the men, therefore that you have under your charge, you are not to treat them as slaves but to manage them as grown-up children – members of your family, who are to be kept in subordination and obedience.'[6]

The Agreement also laid down a scale of daily rations, the provision of a medicine chest and a contract of employment for a particular voyage. The master had overall charge of the rations. If supplies started to run short on a long voyage, he could reduce the daily allowance to ensure there was enough to continue. The Agreement and Account of the Crew was a contract by which all the crew bound themselves under the aforesaid act to serve on the ship in agreed positions, at an agreed wage rate and rations for a specific voyage. By 'signing on' they contracted to 'conduct themselves in an orderly, faithful, honest and sober manner and at all times to be diligent in their respective duties to the lawful Commands of the said Master. . .' The Agreement was accompanied by the *Official Log Book*, in which the master could record acts of indiscipline, accidents, injury, deaths, desertion or other incidents. At the end of the voyage, when the crew were paid off, he also had to make an assessment of the conduct and ability of each sailor. This was recorded in the Agreement and also on the individual's certificate of discharge. A 'decline to report' could hamper a sailor's chances of future employment.

'The entire control of the navigation and working of the ship lies with the master.'[7] He determined the course, coordinated position-finding, and gave all the orders for tacking, wearing and shortening sail, and getting under way. However, under normal conditions the master would delegate much of the detailed running of the ship to his two officers, the mate and second mate (or boatswain), and this included the maintenance of the hull and rigging. He would expect to be consulted whatever the time of day or night about changes of course, sails or anything else of importance. The master would also expect a degree of deference. The weather side of the poop was his place; he did not stand watches, nor did he go aloft except in dire circumstances. He also controlled the main saloon cabin aft with his own 'state room' off it. The chief mate would probably dine with him but apart from that, he had this space to himself. Not only did the master live in splendid isolation but his complete direction of the ship affected everyone else on board: 'He has a power and an influence, both direct and indirect, which may be the means of much good and much evil. If he is profane, passionate, tyrannical and intemperate, more or less of the same qualities will spread themselves or break out among the officers and the men . . . He may make his ship almost anything he pleases, and may render the lives and duties of his officers and men pleasant and profitable to them or may introduce disagreements, discontent, tyranny, resistance.'[8]

After the passage of the Mercantile Marine Act, masters had to hold a certificate of competency, as did the mates. The rest of the crew were qualified by practice, except the carpenter (and the sailmaker if one was carried) who would have served an apprenticeship. The appointment of the officers was in the hands of the master and the owners, while the crew were generally recruited by a shipping master or crimp. The latter would be asked to supply so many men and the master was unlikely to know much about their character or abilities. Occasionally, incompetents could pass themselves off as able seamen. This happened on voyage 19. Liverpool legend has it that Paddy Doyle, a boarding house keeper, 'trained' counterfeit ABs. His tricks included a cow's horn round which the trainee was conducted. This meant he could say in all truth he had been 'round the Horn'! The seamen probably would only come on board at the very last day before sailing. The shipping master, who was usually a sailor's boarding-house proprietor, would be paid a fee and would also take an advance from the seamen's wages, often in return for board and lodgings. The whole business was highly organised in Liverpool to the extent that the boarding-house owners would entice inward-bound crews in the Mersey to go ashore before docking for an early taste of all the delights not available in the forecastle of a sailing ship. The crew on the *Jhelum*'s second voyage were certainly supplied in this way, for a note on the Agreement states: 'crew shipped by John Gillies, 19 Bridgewater Street, Liverpool'.

The *Jhelum*'s total complement was highest – twenty and the master – on voyages 3 to 11. The average was eighteen when she was a full-rigged ship with three square sails on the mizzen mast. After she was cut down to a barque in 1858 this was reduced to fourteen. Her manning was reduced even more after 1865; for example, the second mate's position was taken over by a boatswain and the cook was expected to double as a steward. The crew was made up of first mate, second mate or boatswain (but not both), carpenter, a sailmaker – on only one voyage, steward, cook or cook-steward, able seamen, ordinary seamen, boy and apprentices. The first mate was responsible for the day-to-day management of the ship both at sea and in port, including the overall maintenance of the ship. He also wrote up the log and could act as the master in an emergency. The master could not dismiss him when abroad except in exceptional circumstances.[9] He would not go aloft except in emergencies and was responsible for the anchoring of the ship. At sea he commanded the starboard watch.

The second mate had a much more junior position and commanded the port watch when the master was not on deck. He had to be certified competent in navigation and seamanship to the extent that he could take over the first mate's position in an emergency. Otherwise, he worked aloft and on deck with the crew and in fact was expected to lead by example and be the best seaman on the ship for rigging, etc. If no boatswain or sailmaker were carried, he would look after the stocks of paint, tar, rope, and the spare sails along with the stowage of water and provisions. He might also take responsibility for the weighing and issuing of rations laid down in the Agreement.

The boatswain was an uncertified highly experienced seaman who acted as the foreman of the crew, took charge of the ship's stores and carried out skilled maintenance on the rigging. The carpenter's duty was to work at his trade aboard. He reported to the master and not the mate. He was well paid and in similar vessels to the *Jhelum* lived aft in the steerage. He was in charge of the ship's stock of tools and may have carried his own as well. He was also expected to give a hand with sailing and steering the ship. Like ship's engineers, carpenters served their apprenticeship ashore in a shipyard before going to sea. Three of the *Jhelum*'s carpenters were first voyagers; and one of these, Thomas Rodger, was drowned at Guayaquil on 25th January 1861. The *Official Log* recorded his drowning and a list of his tools. These included 14 caulking irons, 18 chisels, 8 gouges, 12 augers, 3 cold chisels, 2 gauges, 1 horsing iron, 1 stand saw, 1 circular saw, 2 drift bolts, 2 setting stones, 5 hammers of different sizes, 2 squares, 2 bevels, 1 screw driver, 1 saw set, 1 spoke shave, 2 axes, 1 adze, 1 draw knife, 1 soldering iron, 1 maul, 11 moulding and bead planes, 3 hand planes, 2 jack planes, 1 pair of pinchers, 1 pair of pliers, 2 pairs of calipers, 1 pair of dividers, 4 small files, 3 bits, 2 rules and 1 drill.

The steward was the master's servant. He waited on him at table and cleaned the saloon and the cabins. He often issued the food rations. Although he did not stand watches, he was expected to lend a hand on deck. The main sheet was sometimes known as the 'steward's rope' and he would let this go and haul it aft when tacking and wearing. He might also go aloft to help reefing the courses and topsails.

The cook also worked daylight hours, preparing meals for both the officers and the crew. His ingredients were few and often of poor quality. Cooks did not undergo any training. They were quite often either boys, older seamen who had suffered a bad injury or West Indians. They, like the stewards, were expected to help on deck. When tacking or wearing the ship, for example, their station was at the fore-sheet, which was near the galley.

The seamen were divided into three grades, able, ordinary and boys. An able seaman who proved incompetent would be downrated to ordinary seaman, as two hands were on voyage 19. Apart from the boys, who were usually first voyagers, they were all expected to be able to steer the ship and go aloft to handle the sails. The chief test of an able seaman was his ability in the craft of rigging – splicing, serving and so on.

Table 4.1 The origins of 283 of the crews of the *Jhelum*

GREAT BRITAIN	210	74.2%
Scotland	46	
London	26	
Liverpool	21	
Ireland	19	
Wales	14	
Inland	6	
Other English ports	78	
FOREIGN	73	25.8%
Germany	21	(note voyage 8a Hamburg–Liverpool included 9 Germans)
Scandinavia	19	(Sweden 9, Denmark 4, Finland 3, Norway 3)
USA	13	
Others	20	(including Italy, France, Holland, Poland, Portugal, Austria, Belgium, Greece, Canada, Australia, India, China, Peru, St. Vincent, Sierra Leone, Cape Verde).

The origins of 283 of the crews that served in the *Jhelum* are shown in Table 4.1. Three quarters of the crews were British. Some masters recruited men, especially mates, boats and carpenters from their own area. Captain Seymour on voyage 9 brought two young lads as ordinary seamen from Bridport. Perhaps they were relatives or sons of friends. Captain Garrioch had six Scots on voyage 11, including the mate and the carpenter, and four on voyage 13. Captain Stannus from Carrickfergus had four fellow countrymen on voyages 15 and 16, including the mate and the boatswain on voyage 15. Most of them, including the officers, only stayed for the one contracted voyage. There were a few examples of individual able seamen following a particular master to his new ship or small groups of men – probably friends – signing on together.

Desertion at the end of the outward leg of the voyage was common, even though the deserters forfeited their wages to the owners. 'Sunday 11th October 1868, Callao Bay, Thomas Evans and A. Stapman deserted having been taken away by crimps from shore. No effects left, only an empty chest.'[10] It was not perhaps as common on the *Jhelum* as on some other ships of the same period. Her destination ports were not so attractive as, for example, San Francisco or Melbourne in the Gold Rush era. Voyages 10, 13, 15 and 16 had none; and numbers 2, 7, 9, 11 and 17 had two to three. Voyage 3 had twelve, which can be explained by the call at Baltimore on the return leg; voyage 8 saw thirteen desertions at Valparaiso and then desertions of the replacements at Coquimbo. Two more ABs also left to join the Royal Navy at Valparaiso. Voyages 18 and 19 saw six and fourteen desertions and the latter, which will be dealt with in the next chapter, was no doubt brought about by the poor condition of the ship, the lack of numbers and sickness on board. The youth and bachelor state of most sailors might also help to explain their turbulence ashore, their indiscipline afloat and their tendency to desert. The quality of seamen was considered to be a major social problem and Thomas Mackay, a Liverpool shipowner from 1851 to 1871, described seafarers as 'a most abandoned set, living while on shore at the mercy of crimps (shipping masters), and their wages for months mortgaged to redeem the robberies and exactions while in these dens of infamy'.[11] But a shipowner was bound to say that.

Table 4.2 The average ages of the various ranks on board the *Jhelum*

Rank	Average age	Age range
Master (6)	36.7	31–43
Mate (16)	35.6	26–47
2nd Mate (7)	23	21–27
Boatswain (7)	32	26–41
Carpenter (14)	26.7	21–37
Cook (12)	23	19–50
Steward (9)	27.8	18–32
Cook/steward (4)	26.7	20–31
Able seaman (106)★	24.5	17–46
Ordinary seaman (35)	18	15–30
Boys (3)	16	14–17
Apprentices	No ages given	

★ Based on a sample of all the original crews on the outward voyage

Seafaring on the *Jhelum* (and other vessels) was a young man's calling (Table 4.2). Very few Agreements included allotments to those left at home out of the monthly wage (except for officers and carpenters) and this implies that few were married. The casual nature of the employment, single voyage by single voyage, may well have suited their sense of adventure. Desertion was casual and matter of fact in spite of the heavy phrases of the Agreement and desertion had its own rewards. Sailors who were taken on in ports in South America could command a higher monthly rate – perhaps as much as £4 compared with the normal £2 10s.

The master's monthly wages for the *Jhelum* setting out from the United Kingdom were unknown. The prevailing rate suggested that it was probably £10 plus commission on the freight and other accounts, and the 'slop chest' – his own stock of goods for sale to the crew while on passage at high prices and deducted from their wages. For example, on 28th January 1861, the deceased carpenter had bought two pairs of shoes at £1 5s 0d, four shirts at 14s, 2 1/2 lbs of soap at 1s 10d from Captain Garrioch's slop chest. The master might indulge in private trading, although the only evidence for this on the *Jhelum* was the Customs Bills of Entry for Captain Bell's five bundles of carpets and a box of boots from Bombay on the first voyage and Captain Stannus's two log ends of mahogany from Tupilco.[12]

Table 4.3 Monthly wage rates for the crew of the *Jhelum*

Mate	£5–7; £6 was the usual rate, but on the last voyage, Hudson Brough received a reduced rate of £5 while his replacement William Hoole at Callao got £7.
2nd mate	£3–£3 15s, much the junior officer who received less than a more experienced boatswain.
Boatswain	£4
Carpenter	£4–£5 10s
Cook	£2 5s–£4
Cook/steward	£3–£4
Steward	£2 15s–£3
Able seaman	£2 10s–£4 4s
Ordinary seaman	£1–£2 10s, £1 was for a first voyager
Boy	£1– £1 10s

The crew's monthly wage rates (Table 4.3) seem to have prevailed throughout the mid-19th century on sailing ships and were probably higher than many equivalent jobs on land, particularly as food was supplied as well.[13]

The quantity of food was substantial. The quality often left much to be desired. It was issued according to a weekly timetable laid down in the Agreement (Table 4.4). The bread was normally double-baked ship biscuits and the meat salted. No spirits were allowed, and cocoa or chocolate could be substituted for coffee or tea. Molasses could be substituted for sugar. Potatoes, yams, rice or barley could also be issued.

Table 4.4 Timetable of food laid down in the Agreement

Sunday
1lb bread, 1 1/2 lbs salted beef, 1/2 lb flour, 1/8 oz tea, 1/2 oz coffee, 2oz sugar, 3 quarts of water.

Monday
1lb bread, 1 1/4 lbs salt pork, 1/3 pint of peas, 1/8 oz tea, 1/2 oz coffee, 2oz sugar, 3 quarts of water.

Tuesday
1lb bread, 1 1/2 lbs salt beef, 1/2 lb flour, and the same for the other provisions.

Wednesday
1lb bread, 1 1/4 lbs salt pork, 1/3 pint of peas and the same for the other provisions.

Thursday
1lb bread, 1 1/2 lbs beef, 1/2 lb flour, and the same for the other provisions.

Friday
1lb bread, 1¹/₄lbs pork, ¹/₃ pint of peas and the same for the other provisions.

Saturday
1lb bread, 1¹/₂lbs beef, and the same for the other provisions.

Food was cooked in the galley, which was normally a detachable wooden hut lashed on deck in the shelter for the foremast. It had sliding doors so that it could be entered from the lee side and there was usually a coal-fired range for cooking.[14] In bad weather, the galley was often washed out and no hot food or drinks could be made, which increased the misery of all on board. If a deck cargo was carried it could be unlashed and moved. The food once cooked was put into wooden tubs or 'kids' and taken away to the forecastle to be eaten. Every sailor was expected to supply his own utensils, which usually consisted of a tin pot, an iron spoon and his 'jack knife' which served as both fork and carver.

The crew's accommodation, the forecastle, was right in the bows of the *Jhelum*. It was cramped and probably leaky because the foredeck got much heavy usage with the handling of the anchors. As there was no trace of fitted bunks the crew almost certainly slept in hammocks as was the norm for the first half of the 19th century. Hammocks were preferred because it was possible to rig a canvas flysheet over them to protect the sleeper from leaks from the deck.[15] It was not a pleasant place and Lindsay's description of the *Thetis*'s forecastle gives an impression of the *Jhelum*'s sailors' accommodation. The only difference was that the latter had more head room.

The cook, ten seamen, and three apprentices had their abode in the forecastle. This place, which was in the 'tween decks' at the extremity of the bow, may have been about twenty-one feet in width at the after or widest part, tapering gradually away to a narrow point at the stem. The length in midships was somewhere about twenty feet, but much less as the sides of the vessel were approached. The height was five feet from deck to beam, or about five feet nine inches from deck to deck at the greatest elevation between the beams; the only approach to it being through a scuttle or hole in the main deck, about two and a half feet square. Beyond this hole there were no means of obtaining light or ventilation, and in bad weather, when the sea washed over the deck, the crew had to do as best they could without either, or receive the air mixed with spray, and sometimes accompanied by the almost unbroken crest of a wave, which, in defiance of all the tarpaulin guards, too frequently found its way through the scuttle. Here fourteen persons slept in hammocks suspended from the beams, and had their daily food. There was no room for tables, chairs, or stools, so that the tops of their sea-chests in which they kept their clothes and all their possessions, were substituted for those useful and necessary household articles. In fact so closely were these chests packed that it was difficult to sit astride them, the mode which the sailors found most convenient for taking their meals, especially in rough weather. But the whole of this limited space was not appropriated to the use of the crew, for it contained a rough deal locker, in which the beef and soup-kids and other utensils were kept, while the stout staunchions or knight-heads which supported the windlass on the upper deck came through the forecastle, and were bolted to the lower beams; and too frequently, when the ship was very full of cargo, a row of water casks and provisions were stowed along the after-bulkhead, which was a temporary erection; while on the top of these, cables, coils of rope, and numerous other articles were piled. At all times it was a foulsome and suffocating abode, and in bad weather the water and filth which washed about the deck and among the chests and casks created the most intolerable and loathsome stench. Here, however, these fourteen sailors and apprentices slept, washed, dressed, and had their food, except in fine weather, when they took their meals on deck.[16]

Lindsay's account of the *Thetis* suggested that the carpenter berthed aft in a partitioned part of the tween decks known as 'the steerage' under the aft hatch. He would have kept his tools there and presumably had space to work as well. In the *Jhelum* he might have lived in the forward end of the poop, which had its own storage space. The mate and second mate usually had their own cabins, although there was only space for a bunk and a sea chest. There is still much evidence of the cabin's layout aboard the *Jhelum* and this is examined in Chapter 11.

The fit young men of the *Jhelum* do not appear to have suffered unduly from the hard work, and poor food and accommodation. In spite of the heavy cargoes carried on a dangerous stormy route, few major accidents were reported in the *Official Log*. There must have been many minor injuries that were treated by the master with the help of the ship's medicine chest. On voyage 8 there was a case of dysentry and on voyages 11 and 16 individual members of the crew were sent to hospital. On voyage 18, on the 24th June 1868, Alfred Stapman and John Thompson had to be sent from the ship anchored off Buenos Aires to hospital suffering from venereal disease. Voyage 19 saw two other cases that were so bad that the ship had to land them at Rio de Janeiro in September 1869.

On 29th November 1859, while on passage for Valparaiso, at latitude 56° 49' South, longitude 65° 40' West, Robert Halliday, the apprentice, was thrown over the wheel and suffered a dislocated shoulder. The captain tried to relocate the bone, but by the time the ship anchored at Valparaiso on the 28th December the apprentice could not raise his arm. Three doctors examined him and found they could do nothing for him. They reported that he would never be able to raise his arm again. Presumably, this would have ended his career at sea. The heavy gales in the southern latitudes often led to fatalities from accidents or drowning. The crews of the *Jhelum* did not suffer any such casualties nor any falls from the rigging. There were, however, three fatal accidents in port. The carpenter, William Rodger, fell overboard and drowned at Guayaquil in 1861; Baitely Cavanagh slipped and fell overboard at Buenos Aires on Christmas Day 1863 and was not seen again, although there was a boat close at hand; and Bernard Quinn, the cook, fell into the hold and died twenty minutes later when the *Jhelum* was at anchor at Tupilco, Mexico, on 26th July 1866. The *Official Log* gave a revealing list of the contents of his sea chest: 6 pairs of trousers, a cotton frock (like a fisherman's smock), 4 pairs of flannel drawers, 4 pairs of stockings, a blanket, a rug, a mattress, a pillowcase, a looking glass, 3 razors, 2 pairs of shoes, a blue woollen frock, 4 cotton shirts,

3 white flannel shirts, 2 coloured shirts, 2 vests (waistcoats), a pea jacket, 2 comforters (scarves), 2 handkerchiefs, an oilcloth coat and 'sundry trifling articles'. This was little enough for a long voyage or a career at sea.

Notes

1. Seymour was first mate of the *Buenos Ayrean*, 1850–3 and *Anna Henderson*, 1853–4 and captain of the *Helen Wallace*, 1855–8 and *Toftcombs* 1860–3.
2. R.W. Stevens, *On the Stowage of Ships and their Cargoes* (London and Plymouth, 7th edn, 1893), p. 406, quoted in full in Appendix 5.
3. J. Lees, *A Manual for Shipmasters* (Liverpool, 1851), p. 40.
4. W.S. Lindsay, *History of Merchant Shipping and Ancient Commerce* (London, 1874), Vol. 2, p. 501.
5. Lees, *Manual*, p. 14.
6. *Ibid.*, p. 92.
7. Lindsay, *History*, Vol. 2, p. 502.
8. *Ibid.*, p. 506. The Falkland Islands Government archives contains a good description of a tyrannical, drunken master in a letter from the mate of the Glasgow barque *Roebuck* (of similar size to the *Jhelum*) on 12th March 1873 to the Governor in the Inward Correspondence: 'Sir, I am sorry to trouble you again with the affairs of this vessel. Captain Blake came off again tonight drunk and abusing me and the second mate. "You useless hounds. I suppose you are not looking after my stores, you damned scoundrels, you sons of bitches. I will turn you forward to second mate. . . . You bugger I will put you through before we get home for this. . ." This sort of language continued from 6 to 8 o'clock. He having broached a case of brandy, he requested me to drink with him on several occasions, but I refused. Then he would abuse me and cursed in my berth all late events. . .'
9. William Hicks Callow, mate on voyage 8, was discharged by order of a naval court held at Valparaiso on 13th October 1857. Captain Stannus had much trouble with his drunken mate, C. Ransom, on voyage 14. He fined him on many occasions for neglecting his duty, insolent language and absenting himself from the ship for two weeks at St Jago de Cuba and charging his lodgings to the ship's account. For example, he was fined for leaving a boy at the wheel, with the binnacle light out, lying on the skylight and neglecting to brace the yards round as the wind had shifted aft on 25th November 1864. On 27th March 1865 he came into the cabin and told Stannus he was 'a damned Irish pig', 'a shit and no gentleman and he would come knock my bloody head in pieces' etc.
10. *Official Log*, voyage 18.
11. *The Times*, February 19th 1855.
12. *Liverpool Customs Bill of Entry*, April 17th 1850, and *London Customs Bill of Entry*, 16th December 1867.
13. R. Hope, *A New History of British Shipping* (London, 1990), p. 291.
14. B. Greenhill, *The Merchant Schooners* (London, 1957), p. 12.
15. Lindsay, *History*, Vol. 2, p. 535, and see also Chapter 11.
16. Lindsay, *History*, Vol. 2, pp. 497–8.

CHAPTER FIVE

THE LAST VOYAGES

On 23rd March 1863, Joseph Steel junior and William Bell sold the *Jhelum* to Joseph Cunard and James Wilson, shipbrokers of Liverpool. She was due for a major survey. This involved cleaning down the top-side hull planking down to the lightwater mark; the removal of key planks specified in Lloyd's Rules, for example, one in each buttock; and the driving out of certain bolts and treenails. She was found sound and was recaulked, and resheathed with wood along the waterline and yellow metal on felt below. The windlass had been stripped and checked and the anchor chains were up to standard. As a result she was assigned A1 in Red for five years.[1]

The survey was completed and approved by the Lloyd's Committee by 17th July and by then she was in the hands of another shipbroker, Matthew Wilson, who was probably the biggest dealer in ships in Liverpool. He handled the sale of many new Canadian vessels and the American-owned ships that were sold at Liverpool in 1862 and 1863 because of the threat of Confederate commerce raiders like the *Florida* and the *Alabama*. He also traded in Canadian timber and when Barned's bank at Liverpool crashed in March 1866 he had loans amounting to £105,640 on ships and timber.[2] The sale of the *Jhelum*, which was registered on 24th August, was a small transaction for him but clearly a large one for her new joint owners, John Widdicombe and Charles Bell. They immediately sold 21 shares to James Stannus, the new master; 10 to Robert Parry, a Liverpool coal merchant; 4 to William Widdicombe of Cardiff (no doubt a relative of John Widdicombe), master mariner; and 4 to Edwin Moxey, accountant, also of Cardiff. The two managing owners were left with only 24 of the 64 shares.[3]

The *Jhelum*'s outward cargoes and their destinations changed with the new owners. Voyage 14 began on 24th August 1863 from Newport, almost certainly with coal to Buenos Aires. Voyages 15 from Swansea and 18 and 19 from Cardiff also certainly carried coal cargoes, and voyage 16 from Liverpool to Vera Cruz, Mexico, may have carried coal, salt or ballast. The Customs Bills of Entry from 19th January to 14th February 1866 show few exports for Vera Cruz at the time the *Jhelum* was loading and her entry was placed in a separate category as a ship that was loading but not entered. Three other ships for the same destination were entered. Whether the *Jhelum* sailed without cargo or not, the managing owners were short of funds by 16th May 1867 because they raised two mortgages worth £1,000 from C.C. Johnston and J. Yates, 'gentlemen of Liverpool'. She was, however, still sound enough to carry cotton and guano cargoes, both of which demanded a tight ship, and calculated on the value of the shares mortgaged she was worth about £2,700.

Captain Stannus stayed with the vessel for the next two voyages, but both saw trouble with the crew (reduced in numbers), with desertions, hospitalisation and a death. Turnround times increased. She spent almost three months in transit from Callao and loading at the Chincha Islands.[4] This may have been because there were a large number of ships loading guano for the French ports of Dunkirk, Nantes and Le Havre. In the report from the Chinchas for 25th November, 9 ships were listed for Le Havre, 8 for Dunkirk, and 11 for Nantes and Bordeaux.[5] Limited lighterage facilities made loading slow.

The *Jhelum* arrived at Dunkirk on 23rd April 1869. It is not clear how long she took to discharge. Stevens stated that fifteen days, including Sundays, was the time allowed for discharging there for a vessel of the *Jhelum*'s size. She eventually sailed to Cardiff to load coal for Montevideo, probably in May or early June 1869. Captain Stannus left the vessel and on 10th June sold his 21 shares to William Widdicombe, who had moved from Cardiff to 4 Snowdon Street, Smithdown Road, Liverpool, and called himself a shipowner instead of a master mariner. Messrs Widdicombe, C.R. Bell, R. Parry and E.R. Moxey also sold their shares to him and this made him sole owner.

But W.G. Widdicombe and C.R. Bell's shares still carried mortgages on them. The *Jhelum*'s new owner's status as a master mariner turned shipowner was not uncommon in Liverpool at this time. In 1869 he owned the brig *Cambyses* of 254 tons built at South Shields in 1848 and classed in 1867 after a special survey as red A1 for 5 years. He may have also owned the ship *Whirlwind* (834 tons) of Glasgow in the China trade, built at Dundee in 1854 and classed A1 for 9 years from 1863.[6] The *Jhelum*, on the other hand, was out of class and cheap to buy. As a shareholder since 1863 and a professional seaman he must have judged that she was sound enough to continue to carry coal and guano. He financed her purchase by a mortgage of £1,250 at 10 per cent interest to H. Woodall and J.H. Yates of Liverpool. This was a high rate of interest for the time.[7] Almost two months later, on 30th August, he was obliged to take out a second mortgage from D. Dacker and George Offer, shipbrokers of 115 Leadenhall Street, London, to secure his current account. It was not unusual for shipowners to have large borrowings on their ships.[8] Widdicombe also cut down on expenses; for example, he cut the crew to eleven with only five able-bodied seamen and one ordinary seaman. The mate was paid only £5 instead of £6 or £7. He may well have cut down on stores and his credit was not that high because the master was out of funds by the time he reached Montevideo, where he had to take out a bottomry loan of £1,500.[9] The enterprise looks to have been highly opportunist: despatching an old but sound ship for a valuable guano charter in order to clear off all or part of Widdicombe's debts.

Widdicombe's choice of master was intriguing. J.C.G. Beaglehole had left his last ship, the *Kew Kee*, at Shanghai in 1868. She was a composite schooner of 345 tons built and owned in Liverpool in 1864. It is clear from *Lloyd's List* that his old ship was not wrecked, for she continued to be mentioned in the middle of 1869 when Captain Beaglehole was ready to sail for Dunkirk in the *Jhelum*. Perhaps he had been taken ill, perhaps he was dismissed, perhaps it was a delivery voyage. Curiously, *Lloyd's Captain's List* does not mention the *Kew Kee* voyage. He had commanded the 445-ton Liverpool barque *Deogaum* from 1862 to 1865 and from the latter year to 1869 there

Captain William Beaglehole, the elder brother of the master of the *Jhelum*. Family tradition has it that the two brothers resembled each other.

was no reference to any other command. But he must have been experienced, for he had served in five other ships as master going back to his first command, the *John Dalton* in 1856.

John Charles Graham Beaglehole was born in 1827, the son of Henry, mariner and Ann Beaglehole (née Tippett) of Dartmouth. He married Mary Ann Ford at St Petrox Church, Dartmouth, on 4th April 1849. He had an older brother, William Henry, who was also a mariner and who eventually retired from the sea and became a sail-maker. William Henry's portrait survives and family tradition holds that he greatly resembled his younger brother.[10] This is pure speculation, but Widdicombe is a well-known West Country name and it is possible he was related to or acquainted with Beaglehole, and perhaps had been able to offer him employment at a low rate when he was down on his luck. The crew as a whole had a strong West Country element as well: the carpenter and the boatswain were from Padstow, the cook-steward from Bristol, and three able-bodied seamen were from Plymouth, Callington (nearby) and Falmouth. The mate, Hudson Brough, had served with the boatswain on the *Witch of the Wave*, a 277-ton barque built at Teignmouth in 1853 and owned by Guthrie and Co of Liverpool. At 48 he was old for a mate and as it turned out was not in the best of health.

The *Jhelum* sailed from Cardiff on 30th June 1869 bound for Rosario; and had to put into Rio de Janeiro on 20th September. *Lloyd's List* stated that she was 'leaky'. There had already been trouble on the voyage with William Heggery, which was recorded in the *Official Log Book*.[11] On the 1st July he refused to grease down the mizzen topmast and was later found by the mate asleep in the forecastle when he was supposed to be on watch. From the subsequent entries, he may have had reason, for he and Albert Sayers were sent to the hospital at Rio on 25th September suffering from syphilis. Sayers discharged himself on 3rd October from hospital and was found wandering in the street. He refused to stay in hospital because he could not stand the mercury treatment. Neither he nor Heggery returned to the ship. If they had, they would have found that the master had disrated them to ordinary seamen, describing them as 'the most useless and ignorant men, of an able seaman's duty, fit only for an ordinary rating and scarcely deserving that'.

Captain Beaglehole was not alone in expressing his poor opinion of his sailors. Captain Stap of the *Great Britain*, for example, in 1883, wrote 'and a more useless lot I never was with, half a dozen of them no sailors at all, substitutes slipped on board at the last moment with only what they stood up in and are no earthly use on board'.[12] The *Jhelum*'s crews, and they were replaced twice, seemed to be of similar quality. On the 2nd and 3rd October the remaining seamen deserted. This may have reflected both the conditions on board and the temptations of Rio. There was no problem in finding another six replacements, who signed on at a higher rate of pay (£3 as against £2 10s a month) on 15th October, four days before sailing for Montevideo for orders.

Three of them, George Harding, aged 24, William Cargel, 23, and John Slater, 24, were survivors of the wreck of the *Royal Standard* of Liverpool, an iron ship of 2,033 tons built as an auxiliary passenger ship in 1863 for the original White Star Line and converted to sail in 1867. She went ashore near San Thomé on 10th October 1869. The *Jhelum* and her master were not to their liking. George Harding was 'logged' for answering the master in 'the most mutinous and disrespectfull manner that can be imagined'. On 5th November, and when the ship came to anchor off Montevideo on 13th he refused to work and demanded to see the British Consul. Two days later he and the rest of the crew deserted. It is likely that the *Jhelum* was towed the 350 miles to Rosario, and as a result the deserters were not replaced until she was ready to sail for Callao. Hudson Brough, the mate, was paid off at Rosario on 29th November because he was too ill to withstand the rigours of a Cape Horn Passage and was replaced at Montevideo by an acting mate, William Scott.

As it was the low water season at Rosario, the *Jhelum* discharged her coal at anchor into lighters, and at 4.30 in the morning of 14th November she was hit by a 'pampero', the violent wind characteristic of the river Plate, parted her port cable, hit a Dutch brig and the British barque *Roxana*,[13] and suffered 'considerable damage to rigging and bulwarks'. It was this incident that obliged the master to take out a bottomry bond or loan on the security of the ship to carry out repairs. This was a very serious matter and only undertaken in the direst emergency. It could lose the owners their vessel and the master would be held responsible. The terms of Beaglehole's bottomry bond are not known but the seriousness of such a loan can be appreciated from one documented in the archives of Merseyside Maritime Museum that was taken out by Joshua Rowe, master of the barque *Russell* (342 tons) at Bahia, Brazil, on 1st December 1886. Rowe borrowed £600 at 30 per cent interest to carry out repairs and pledged himself and his heirs, the ship, freight money and cargo as security.[14]

On 4th February, the *Jhelum* was at Montevideo. William Vincent had been signed on as sailmaker. This was a unique appointment and perhaps the sails needed repairing before reaching the stormy waters off Cape Horn. Two days later, seven seamen were taken on, with Joseph Avery completing the crew on 8th March. The hire of additional hands suggests that the master was expecting a difficult passage, because the ship was in poor condition. This is confirmed by the fact that on 5th March, the carpenter, the cook-steward and four able bodied seamen petitioned the British Consul to arrange a survey of the ship because they considered her unseaworthy. The survey was carried out by two captains and a shipwright who reported 'most favourably on the ship . . . nothing was wrong and she could pursue her voyage to Callao'. The expenses for detaining the ship amounted to £32 10s. The survey cost 48 dollars which was deducted from the wages of the six who had made 'the vexatious and frivolous complaint'. She probably sailed in ballast.

On 17th March at latitude 48° 20' South, longitude 62° 40' West, Alexander Gunn was 'logged': 'for swearing while getting the sails out of the hold to air. A sail got foul and he began to curse and Jesus. I told him to be quiet. He said the ship was very religious. I said he should not make use of such words in my presence. He said it was my time now but his was to come and then he would have me.' The report was witnessed by the mate and the passenger, a Mr Pye, and the mate had to send Gunn out of the cabin to stop his abusive language. Beaglehole also added that Gunn had been found sick on many occasions but he could not detect any symptoms of illness. On 28th March, at 58° South, 43° 28' West, lime juice and vinegar were issued to the crew, '20 days out and four fresh meat days in the interval'.

One of the able-bodied seamen taken on at Montevideo, Joseph Dean, went aft, troubled by an old wound from an accident on another ship. The master poulticed it and noted the incident in the *Log* on 7th April. Two weeks later, when the ship was to depart from Callao for the Guanape islands to load guano after being surveyed to meet the demand of the charter party, Joseph Dean was discharged as unfit to continue. Two other seamen were also discharged and four were taken on for the return trip between Callao and Guanape to load the guano. The *Jhelum* was only one of a large number of ships loading guano for French ports at the islands. *Lloyd's List* for 1st August listed 39 vessels in May and June there, of which 31 were bound for France.

The loading by lighter was slow and the *Jhelum* did not get back to Callao for clearance until 6th July. Six days later she set sail for France with a new mate, William Hoole, on £7 a month; another able-bodied seaman, William Daws; an ordinary seaman, James Altass; and a first voyager boy, Henry Andrews, aged 15. What an introduction for him to life at sea the rest of the voyage was to be! Because of the equinoctial gales it was a bad time of the year to be making the passage for any vessel, let alone an old one. Guano was a difficult enough cargo when dry and far worse when wet. It was customary to load the cargo on a wooden platform laid about 2 feet above the keelson and well clear of the sides of the ship. There would have been a first layer of part-filled bags with the remainder tipped in in bulk. On some ships the tween deck planks were removed to ensure that the pile was a consolidated whole. The archaeological survey suggests that the *Jhelum*'s tween deck planking was removed because it was of little use for bulk cargoes such as guano and coal. Some ships had the guano coated with a skin of plaster or used dilute sulphuric acid to form a crust on it. This reduced the terrible ammonia fumes and helped protect the cargo from water. Guano was not usually loaded right in the bow or the stern; stowing usually started aft of the foremast.

Stevens, who has much to say on guano cargoes, quotes examples of what could happen if they got wet. On 31st October 1857, the barque *Victor* left the Chinchas with 600 tons; she then began to leak fore and aft and the crew had to pump her out. Loose guano frequently choked the pumps and the waterways. Water at the stem and the stern had to be bailed out by the crew who 'suffered severely from the effects on the skin of their hands and by the ammonia which escaped more readily when the cargo was wetted'. Wet guano could also behave in another dangerous way; it could cake into one lump. As one master graphically put it: 'the guano moved about like a lump of ice in a bucket of water', making a ship unstable especially when she went about.[15] The *Jhelum*'s condition seems to have been similar to the *Victor*'s. Captain Beaglehole had jettisoned some of the cargo, but most of it must have remained in good dry condition, because a ship was chartered to complete its delivery.[16] It was a valuable cargo. If the prevailing price was £13 a ton and the *Jhelum* had 500 tons, which was the quantity she had carried on voyage 9, she would have had a cargo worth £6,500. At modern rates this might be about £660,000.[17] Even though it was reported that some of the cargo had been jettisoned, it could not have been much because a short-handed crew would have had great difficulty shifting a large amount of fuming guano in a gale. The total cargo could not have been worth less than £300,000 in today's money.

On 18th August the *Jhelum* anchored at Stanley in a foundering state. The ship was strained and leaking, there were no funds to repair her and the crew were exhausted. Beaglehole wrote in the *Official Log*: 'Barque *Jhelum* put into this port in distress having experienced heavy gales during the passage made her leak and damage part of the cargo and considered not safe to proceed further on her voyage. The damages sustained and making 14 inches of water per hour at sea and no funds to repair in consequence of the breaking up of the voyage.' She was not the only vessel to have suffered. When Governor D'Arcy wrote to London in October 1870 he reported that eight ships had sought refuge because of the weather. They included the *Astricana*, with one man lost, other crew injured and spars damaged; the schooner *Vampyr*, which failed to weather the Horn, 84 days out of London; the American ship *Madawska* from New York for Portland, with three men lost, and boats and cabin stove in; and the *Vicar of Bray*, 133 days out from London with bulwarks and boats gone, and the captain and crew carried ashore worn out with exposure. The Governor was not slow to point out the value of Stanley. 'Thus my Lord within the space of one month this harbour has afforded rescue to eight vessels and it would be an interesting matter of record to detail to your lordship at some future opportunity the numerous occasions when this Harbour of Refuge has been of the greatest utility to the Imperial Merchant Marine.'[18] D'Arcy was incorrect in one detail: he stated that the *Jhelum* had been condemned, but it was not that simple.

At 8.30 in the morning of 31st August the crew and the officers told Captain Beaglehole that they would not continue the voyage. The vessel had to be surveyed to prove whether or not she was seaworthy. This was routine with distressed ships at Stanley.[19] On 3rd September, the Governor appointed a surveyor who pronounced

Stanley harbour, March 1871. The damaged *Vicar of Bray* was anchored on the extreme left. HMS *Galatea* lies beyond the hulk to the left of centre in the distance. The stern of the *Jhelum* is visible on the extreme right. The hulk at the end of the jetty is the *Actaeon*.

the ship unseaworthy and the master, having no funds to carry out repairs, made arrangements to discharge the crew to reduce his expenses. They were paid by bills of exchange drawn on the owner's account and not in cash. Two went on 14th September and the remaining six on 4th October, leaving the carpenter, the cook-steward, the mate and Henry Nelson, the apprentice.

Captain Beaglehole was not a free agent. His prime duty was to the owners, not the crew. As 'a common carrier' he was bound to make every effort to try and deliver the cargo to Dunkirk. Only then would the owners receive the bulk of the freight money. Masters were enjoined not to sell the ship or the cargo and to be wary of Lloyd's Agents, who could put owners to extra expenses. The alternatives seemed to be either to refit the ship or to charter a second vessel to collect the cargo.[20] But Beaglehole had no funds. He needed a decision from the owner. There were other interested parties; the insurers and owners of the cargo, and F.E. Cobb, the manager of the Falkland Islands Co and local agent for Lloyd's. The FIC was not in a good financial position and always short of cash. Ship repair, provisioning and agency work were useful sources of income. He faced stiff competition from Dean & Co for this kind of work. As he wrote to the FIC directors in London: 'While away at Darwin, a number of vessels came in which the company had a poor share . . . the *Jhelum* with guano is to be paid and Derbyshire of Montevideo consulted as they hold a bottomry of £1500 on her and the last survey condemns her.' The lender of a bottomry loan would lose his money if the voyage were not completed. His letter continued: 'I got Captain Scales to survey her and he recommends to caulk and? The men complained to the Governor and he appointed another survey which declared her not fit to go to sea. Captain Beaglehole then called another and they condemned her as likely to cost over her value in repairs. What will be done eventually I do not know.'[21]

Captain Scales was a Lloyd's surveyer who had been sent out to deal with the wreck and cargo of the ship *Balcarry*.[22] Cobb decided to extend credit to the *Jhelum*'s master but was worried about her and the *Vicar of Bray*: 'I think you would do well to hunt up the owners of this vessel and the *Jhelum* and secure any further business, they may do here, making money matters all right and sending me full instructions'.[23] Cobb advanced Beaglehole a total of £106 15s and seems to have cut off his credit in about February or March 1871 when it began to become clear that he was unlikely to get his company's money back.

On 24th December Beaglehole reduced his costs further by discharging the steward and the carpenter because they were able to find paid work ashore. Word of the *Jhelum*'s condition must have got through to her owners and insurers because by December the iron barque *Pelham* of London (340 tons) had been chartered at Le Havre to go and pick up the guano. She was reported to be loading by the Salvage Association on 11th January and to be ready to sail ten days later.[24] Meanwhile Cobb attempted to get his directors to contact her owners, which they clearly had not done: 'Captain Coleman of the *Vicar of Bray* is dead and that vessel and the *Jhelum* both wait for orders to which I hope you have attended.'[25] It looks as if Widdicombe had deliberately not responded and it may be that the *Pelham*, which he should have chartered in order to collect the freight money, was hired by the insurers of the guano cargo. By 30th January, Beaglehole was thinking of selling the ship but Cobb advised him to wait to hear what his owners said.[26] He was occasionally mentioned in the Government records. He subscribed five shillings to an appeal for the All Saint's Sisterhood in aid of their work in nursing the sick and wounded in the battlefield on the 14th December 1870. On 10th February 1871 he explained to the Governor that he could not carry out the harbour master's request to move the *Jhelum* because he had insufficient crew and no funds to hire extra labour; on the 18th, he assisted Captain Scales to survey cargo recovered from the wreck of the schooner *Lotus*.

HMS *Galatea*, commanded by HRH Alfred, the Duke of Edinburgh, arrived in Stanley on the 24th February; four days later Captain Beaglehole wrote to Henry Byng, the Falklands' Colonial Secretary and Shipping Master: 'Situated as I am without means to release my ship from her liabilities or food for my mate and self, Captain Scales prohibiting the sale of the ship after six surveys proving her unseaworthy, will you kindly oblige in assisting me by appointing if possible a survey by some efficient officers of the *Galatea* to prove whether or not the ship is in a fit state to proceed on her voyage.'[27] His request was granted and the staff commander and carpenter of the *Galatea* carried out the survey, reporting that the outside planking and copper was generally defective and needed to be refastened; the upper iron breasthook was broken at the throat bolt (this fracture can still be seen on the ship); and that many internal timbers were decayed or broken. The iron stanchions in the hold were bent and loose and this had caused the upper deck to sink at the waist and at the break of the poop. The deck planking was defective, the main hatchway beams were broken, and the bulwarks needed general repairs. All this work would have to be carried out before she could put to sea again.[28] Nothing immediately happened as a result of this apparently damning survey. On 29th March, Byng wrote to an unknown correspondent requesting him to advance £50 to Beaglehole's family in Dartmouth. He mentioned that Beaglehole was owed between £150 and £190.[29] And still the unfortunate master was left with the *Jhelum*. It would have probably been legitimate by the end of April 1871 for Beaglehole to have sold the *Jhelum*, but just as he was about to do so, Cobb, in his capacity as Lloyd's Agent, received an urgent letter from Mr Harper, an underwriter in London, protesting about her possible sale. This would have been either Samuel or J.A.W. Harper, who were listed as members of Lloyd's in the subscriber's list of the 1869 *Register*. It is not clear why Harper should have wanted to prevent the sale, but it appears to have been a matter concerning the cargo. Unfortunately Cobb's copy of his letter to his directors has been obscured through age: 'No answer received as to the *Jhelum* or the *Vicar of Bray*, but I got an urgent letter from Mr. Harper requesting me to stop the sale of the former which I effectually prevented. [Some(?)] were his cargo. The captain goes home ship mail to see his owners.'[30]

On 4th May 1871, Beaglehole wrote again to the Governor requesting permission to sail to Liverpool to try and settle matters with his uncommunicative owner: 'It is utterly impossible to obtain funds to defray expenses of the vessel and the crew, the merchants having refused to advance money on the ship. I have come to the conclusion that the only plan left for me is to go home. If your Excellency would kindly agree that I may leave for England in the barque *Eagle*, I am willing to sign a guarantee for the amount charged for the passage money for the said vessel.'[31] Cobb also pressed the Governor for a decision: 'With reference to our conversation of yesterday on the subject of the *Jhelum*, I beg leave to repeat that the sole impediment in the way of Captain Beaglehole in the difficulty of leaving the ship as neither J.M. Dean & Son nor I wish to act as agents – my reason being I act for underwriters in the matter. I therefore suggest that the vessel be left in the charge of the government which will afford a guarantee against improper proceedings and the master will be enabled to bring matters to a conclusion at home . . . Should the *Jhelum*'s affairs be settled a *great discredit* to the port will be removed.'[32]

Governor D'Arcy agreed and J.M. Dean & Co were persuaded to act for the *Jhelum*. Captain Beaglehole, the mate, the steward-cook and the carpenter appeared before a panel consisting of the Governor, the Chairman of the Council, and Byng to decide what to do about the *Jhelum* and the remaining crew. The government was already supplying them with food and lodgings and it was agreed that they should all be sent back to England because it was impossible to get funds to pay them at Stanley. The mate refused to accept a bill of exchange drawn on the owners because he doubted it was valid and continued to do so until the final entry in the *Jhelum*'s *Official Log* on 24th May.[33] Captain Beaglehole did not sail in the *Eagle*, but in HMS *Charybdis*, which left on or about 28th May 1871.[34]

Beaglehole's final entry in the Log was on Saturday May 27th: 'The mate, Mr. Hoole, still refuses his discharge but accepts his bill on the owners under protest, he doubting its validity. At the same time, before the shipping master, still claims to remain on the articles and receive his wages up to the time of the Board of Trade finally settling it in England. We leave this place in HMS *Charybdis* having no further credit in this place for further sustinance, there being no alternative.' Four days earlier, Byng had written to the Assistant Secretary of the Marine Department of the Board of

Trade in London, outlining the situation of the master, mate, carpenter and cook-steward.

> The Captain although he wrote repeatedly to his owners could not obtain answers to his letters and was compelled to discharge the greater part of his crew retaining however the services of the first mate, the carpenter and the steward who elected to remain by the ship considerable wages being due to them. But as nearly a year elapsed on and no instructions were received (only a protest from the underwriters against the sale of the vessel) it became necessary to forward these men also to the United Kingdom as distressed British subjects, the Master being unable to get their wages by payment in cash, the bills he was desirous of giving impossible to cash in their settlement and as the winter was again coming when work is difficult to obtain, they became absolutely destitute and I afforded them relief. As the amount of their bills on the owners Messrs. Widdicombe and Bell is greater than the expenses I incurred on their behalf, all particulars of the form C6 are forwarded on this opportunity together with their bills.'[35]

This was not quite the end of the affair. No record survives of Beaglehole's meetings with Widdicombe on his return to Liverpool. The *Official Log* has one post-script. The Registrar General of Shipping and Seamen at London sent a request to the superintendent of his branch office in Liverpool on 18th May 1871 asking for the return of List C (the *Log*) for the *Jhelum*, as she had been condemned. The Liverpool superintendent wrote back: 'The owner says he is not aware of the vessel being condemned' and the stamp on the same page states 'ship's report received 9 March 1872'. The owner was correct, for according to the *Liverpool Shipping Register* the *Jhelum* was not finally condemned until 30th September and this register closed on 4th October 1871. The question remains as to why Widdicombe did not communicate with his captain. He must have been aware of her arrival in distress at Stanley. Perhaps he was hoping that the damage could be patched up. Perhaps he was overwhelmed by a second disaster, for the *Cambyses*, his other ship, had sunk off Madeira with all hands in August 1870.[36]

Widdicombe's business does not seem to have survived long after the *Jhelum* disaster, for his name disappeared from the local trade directories after 1873 and if, as seems likely, the *Whirlwind* was his ship, he sold her in 1875. The *Jhelum* herself was still afloat in Stanley and in the hands of Dean & Co. Cobb, in his letter to the Governor, had stated that she could be kept afloat by being pumped out once a week. This may have been true, for once she was relieved of the strain of sailing and the deadweight of the guano, her leaks would have been reduced. It is likely that Dean used her for a time as a floating warehouse, for there was always a shortage of covered space to store wool clip, coal or the cargoes of damaged ships. The FIC accounts carried forward the debt owed by Beaglehole until 1874, again a pointer to Widdicombe's disappearance or bankruptcy. In July that year, there is payment by Dean for £32 0s 6d to set against the debit of £106 15s, and the account was closed with a loss of £74 14s 6d.[37] Dean had the power of attorney from the master, FIC was the Lloyd's agent and as the vessel was condemned, the FIC could claim on the proceeds of the sale of the ship. Unfortunately, neither Dean's nor Packe's records are available; but it looks as if the

Jhelum was sold in 1874 to the Packe brothers. According to *Lloyd's Captain's List,* Captain Beaglehole commanded the *Ling Lai* between 19th January 1872 and 16th May 1873, and the *British Nation* between 15th August 1876 and 22nd October 1877. He disappeared from the record thereafter.

Notes

1. *Lloyd's Register Survey* no. 18262, National Maritime Museum, London.
2. M.K. Stammers, *The Passagemakers*, (Brighton, 1978), p. 220.
3. *Liverpool Register of Shipping*, no.351/1863, see Appendix 2.
4. R.W. Stevens, *On the Stowage of Ships and their Cargoes* (London and Plymouth, 7th edn, 1893), p. 293. The charter party used by the English agents of the Peruvian Guano Consignment Co. stipulated 10 running days per 100 tons of new register measurement, which meant that the *Jhelum*, which was permitted to load about 500 tons of guano, would have been allowed a month. Ships loading guano had to call at Callao to be inspected and if necessary have their decks and hull planking recaulked before being allowed to proceed to the Chinchas or Guanape Island. This whole charter party is in Appendix 4. The large shipment to France is interesting. Guano seemed to be less popular by this time with British farmers.
5. *Lloyd's List*, January 2nd 1869.
6. *Lloyd's Register of British and Foreign Shipping* (1869).
7. Sir William Forwood noted that: 'We had a money panic almost every ten years, 1847, 1857, 1866 of the severity of which we can form little idea. It was not merely that the bank rate advanced to eight, nine or even ten per cent but it was impossible to get money at any price.' quoted in Stammers, *Passagemakers*, p. 65.
8. James Baines & Co of Liverpool, for example, had over £600,000 of loans with Barneds Bank when it crashed in 1866, and numerous other examples are to be found in the *Liverpool Ship Registers*. See Stammers, *Passagemakers*, pp. 74, 220.
9. Falkland Islands Co. Archives, Cobb to Directors, FIC, London, 3rd October 1870.
10. Information from S.F. Beaglehole, Paignton, and *Lloyd's Captain's Lists*, Guildhall Library, London.
11. *Official Log*, 1869–71, held at Memorial University, Newfoundland.
12. Quoted in D. Walker, *Champion of Sail, R.W. Leyland and his Shipping Line* (1986), p. 101.
13. It is uncertain which ship this was, *Lloyd's Register* for 1869 has only a steamer and a coasting brigantine of that name.
14. Alsop Wilkinson Collection, Merseyside Maritime Museum.
15. Stevens, *On the Stowage of Ships*, p. 297.
16. *Lloyd's List*, October 29th 1870.
17. W.M. Matthew, 'Peru and the British Guano Market, 1840–1870', *Economic History Review*, vol. XXIII, p. 117. It is very difficult to transfer 1870s volumes in modern prices. This is my estimate based on 'the exchange rate' used for the late 19th century at the Lloyd's Bank, Blist's Hill Museum, Ironbridge, in 1991.
18. Falklands Islands Government Archives, despatches, 15th October 1870, Governor D'Arcy to Rt Hon. Earl of Kimberley.
19. The FIG Archives contain a number of other examples, e.g., inward correspondence 14th November 1872, petition of the crew of the British ship *Oxford*.
20. J. Lees, *A Manual for Shipmasters* (Liverpool, 1851), pp. 190, 195; *Sea Breezes*, new series, vol. III, pp. 222–5.
21. FIC Archives, F.E. Cobb to Directors, London, 641, 3rd October 1870.
22. FIG Archives, inward correspondence, 18th February 1871.
23. FIC Archives, F.E. Cobb to Directors, London, 654, 17th October 1870.
24. *Lloyd's List*, 24th December 1870 and 22nd March 1871.
25. FIC Archives, F.E. Cobb to Directors, London, 685, 10th January 1871.
26. *Ibid.*, 720, 30th January 1871.

27.   FIG Archives, inward correspondence, 28th February 1871.
28.   FIG Archives, 2nd March 1871, see Appendix 6.
29.   FIG Archives, 29th March 1871.
30.   FIC Archives, F.E. Cobb to Directors, London, 2nd May 1871.
31.   FIG Archives, inward correspondence, 4th May 1871.
32.   FIC Archives, F.E. Cobb to Governor D'Arcy, 4th May 1871.
33.   *Official Log*, 16, 4th May 1871.
34.   FIG Archives inward correspondence, 26th May 1871, Captain of HMS *Charybdis* to Governor D'Arcy.
35.   FIG Archives, despatches 24th May 1871.
36.   *Lloyd's Library, Casualties Book*, 22nd August 1870 in Guildhall Library, London.
37.   FIG Archives, Ledger 1870–1.

PART TWO

INVESTIGATIONS OF THE HULK OF THE *JHELUM*
1987–90

CHAPTER SIX

THE SURVEY
PROGRAMME, GENERAL
HULL CONDITION AND
LAYOUT

THE SURVEY PROGRAMME

Work on surveying the *Jhelum* was carried out during three two-week field trips in January and November 1987 and January 1990. The author made a second visit in June 1990 to assist the Falklands Museum and this provided another opportunity to check some key measurements in the hold. The first objective was to produce an accurate plan of the lines of the *Jhelum*. Having established that important overall framework, a second objective was the detailed recording of individual components or structures. The field records have been incorporated into a series of plans. Measurements and excavation were accompanied by a detailed photographic survey. There were many problems with the survey because the *Jhelum*'s structure was large, complex, and partly distorted and dismantled. The vessel had a list to port of about 20 degrees. The position of many major fittings which were missing, such as the masts, had to be determined by careful examination of timber fragments, mortises and other remains. The study of contemporary shipbuilding practice recorded in archival and printed sources helped to unravel some of these problems.

Access to the wreck was by a decaying wooden jetty. This had to be negotiated with care, especially in gales and at high tide. Much of the structure of the *Jhelum*, especially in the forward section, was in a dangerous condition. Time had to be spent taking down loose timbers such as sections of the port and starboard rails, and rigging stagings and crawling boards. The hold was only accessible at low tide and was a mess of loose timber, rocks, mud, glass and seaweed. The almost constant wind and the very variable weather occasionally held up work, especially in the work boat. The recording programme was kept as flexible as possible and was integrated with the stabilisation work to make the most use of limited time and a small workforce.

Work on the outside of the wreck was carried out from the *Mermaid*, a 12-foot fibreglass work boat propelled either by oars or by a 5hp outboard motor. She was built at Fiddlers Ferry boatyard near Warrington and paid for by the Friends of Merseyside Maritime Museum. She was shipped to Port Stanley in advance of the January 1987 field visit courtesy of Hogg Robinson & Co, shipping agents to the Falklands Government. She is housed in the Government boathouse, cared for by Falklands Conservation and used to monitor the condition of all the historic ship-wrecks in Port Stanley harbour.

There was no survey, specification or plan for the *Jhelum* at the time of her launch in 1849. The *Liverpool Registrar of Shipping's Curve Book* of 1856 contains a set of internal sections of her hold. This survey was carried out to recalculate the ship's tonnage for registry according to the new rules laid down in the Merchant Shipping Act of 1854. These were useful when drawing up the lines. There are two *Lloyd's Register Surveys*, numbers 18262 and 27950 for 1863 and 1866, at the National Maritime Museum, Greenwich.[1] The first contains detailed information on the dimensions, types of timber and fastenings in the hull. Survey measurements generally coincided with those of the Lloyd's Surveyor. It was useful for confirm-ing the dimensions of weathered, missing or inaccessible timbers. It also contained useful information about fittings, anchors and sails. The second was less detailed because it was a survey after repairs had been completed and not a reclassification. It established the fact that the *Jhelum* needed repairs and the length of her stay in London.

In 1978, Norman Brouwer of the South Street Seaport Museum, New York, and M.K. Stammers, who were both members of the South Street Seaport–National

The *Jhelum* in 1888, enlarged from a photo-graph taken by Schulz. The corrugated iron roof over the stern section can be clearly seen.

Maritime Historical Society expedition to the Falklands of 1978, began compiling a list of measurements of the more accessible parts of the *Jhelum*. These have been incorporated in the present description after checking. In 1983 Mensun Bound of Oxford University's MARE undertook a condition report for the Falkland Islands' Government, and in 1984 Tim Parr of the Maritime Trust carried out another condition report funded by the Falkland Islands Foundation and Merseyside County Council. The latter included recommendations for first-aid conservation and long-term preservation.

The present survey started in January 1987 with a pre-disturbance survey to record the differences in the fill of the hold. The positions of loose timbers in the hold were not recorded because they were shifted by each high tide. After careful consideration, the work to establish the lines of the hull was carried out mainly from inside the ship. The problems of accurately measuring the exposed starboard side were considerable and measuring time would have been much reduced by the vagaries of the weather. All the measurements were to the starboard side of the hull, which was more exposed because of the vessel's list.

Because the hull had distorted considerably over its length, with the forward bow section leaning further to port than the after section, and because of a possible hog in the keel, lifting accurate measurements for lines was very difficult. The fact that the bottom of the vessel was submerged and filled with rock and other debris and that even at low water the top of the keelson was about 4 feet under the surface added to the difficulty. Because of the distortion, setting up a fore and aft centreline and measuring from it would not have helped to produce accurate lines, though such a line was set up from the centre of the apron to the centre of the sternpost. This line was to check both transverse and longitudinal distortion, by measuring from the line to both keelson and centres of beams.

Measurements from which a lines plan of the *Jhelum* was produced were lifted from the vessel using the following methods. At ten different locations along the centreline of the ship a wooden straight-edge was set up. The straight-edge was fixed in position against both main deck and hold beams, which were one above the other. In the forward section, where most hold beams were missing, main deck beams alone were used. The edge of the board was fixed in line with the exact centre of both beams. An additional check for accuracy was made by centring the edge with the metal stanchion fixed between the hold beam and the keelson. The straight-edge was marked with lines (waterlines), 2 feet apart, with one of the lines located level with the underside of the hold beam. This was repeated at each location in order to give uniform location points at each measuring position when producing the lines plan.

A large wooden T-square and a 45° set square were used to take a series of measurements from each waterline to the ceiling. The square was fixed in turn at each waterline and a long measuring batten slid along its upper edge until it touched the vessel's side. This produced a series of accurate waterline measurements. The same method was used with the set square, producing diagonal measurements.

Where possible, buttock measurements were taken by ramming a measured steel bar down through the rubble to the ceiling. This was done at 2-, 4- and 6-foot distances from the centreline. Measurements were then taken from the bar to a waterline. Because of the amount of rubble and rocks in the vessel, this was possible only at

The starboard bow, 1987. The forward section of the rail and the cathead are still in position. Note also the complicated compound structure of the stem or knee of the hold. The aperture cut for the WC is clearly visible along with the steel anchor plates of the wire ropes. A portion of the wooden sheathing can be seen below these. The large area of missing planking in the 'splash zone' and the list in the forward section caused by the loss of the deck beams indicate the vulnerability of the hulk.

a few locations. In fact at several locations it was possible only to lift a few waterline/diagonal measurements, and these only to the upper portion of the vessel.

Each location, with its individually and accurately placed perpendicular centreline, ensured measurements largely unaffected by the vessel's overall distortions. This method in effect produced a grid comprising waterlines, diagonals and buttocks, just as used when designing a vessel on paper, only in the reverse order.

A further set of measurements was taken forward and aft where shape was extreme and altered rapidly. This was done by setting up a long straight-edge about 30 feet in length horizontally from the centre line of the back of the apron/sternpost to a point where a deck-beam met the side. The straight-edge was marked into 2-foot sections. Using a large square, a series of measurements was taken from the straight-edge to the inside surface of the ship at each marked section. This method was particularly helpful in recording the shape of the rail forward. This operation was repeated at a series of parallel levels both forward and aft. The resulting measurements, in conjunction with the waterlines, diagonals and buttocks, enabled the production of as accurate a set of lines as one could wish for, given the circumstances. The vessel's curves, from the *Curve Book*, were also used as a further check. The first *Curve Book* section was taken some 20 feet from the stem and gave little indication of shape in the bows. The forward shape was therefore determined from the measurements detailed above.

The *Jhelum* had become distorted, not only along the centreline, but along the whole starboard side and especially in the bows. This was mainly because of a combination of the list to port and the absence of most of the main deck and hold beams. The resultant loss of transverse support had caused a sagging of the starboard side from break of poop to stem. Much of her hull was submerged and out of reach. A lot of information concerning the precise shape of submerged components such as keelson, deadwoods, forefoot, etc. and exactly how they were fitted and jointed to each other was not discovered. For example, the sheer of the vessel was calculated by using a combination of the known depth of hold amidships, the known draught forward and aft, and measurements taken to the top of stem and top of sternpost from the respective draught marks. Because both main and tween decks are parallel with each other, one can only assume that the top of the keelson rose both forward and aft, thus transferring sheer to the upper part of the vessel. In fact, the determination of the sheer and the actual overall height of the *Jhelum* proved difficult. The draught marks, both forward and aft, when combined with the known dimensions of keel, floors and keelson and the depth of hold amidships, produced a measurement 2 feet less than expected. The initial survey had indicated a ship with no sheer at all. This was assumed after the hold and tween deck stanchions were in each area found to be exactly the same length throughout the vessel. This, coupled with the assumption that the keelson was straight and not curved, indicated no sheer. A dive was made aft, resulting in the location of a false keel some 11 inches wider. Measurements taken from the bottom of the false keel to the No. 8 draught mark gave a measurement of 18 feet exactly, confirming

Starboard view from the stern quarter. This shows the damage caused by the fire of 1983. The condition of the fore end with the missing planking is dramatically highlighted from this angle.

Inside view of the fore-hold from the loading port. The timber in the right-hand foreground is the port side of the headledge of the main hatch. Only hold beam HC is still intact. It has been covered with marine plywood to protect its upper face. The timber 'props' to stabilise the starboard side are on the right of the picture. Note also the fill of the fore-hold – mud, rock and loose timbers – and the ship's windlass.

our view that the 8 feet mark represented 18 feet. Further measurements taken from the draught marks to both top of stem and top of sternpost indicated a sheer rise of 1 foot forward and 9 inches aft. This resolved the problem of the 'missing' 2 feet.

Further measurements were taken of all the main structural features and their individual components. These included the bow, stern together with the frames, deck beams, knees, shelves, and waterways, planking and ceiling. The most complex structure was the stern. The internal structure had to be measured in the hold separately, in the poop accommodation, on the poop deck above and from the water. Deck and rigging fittings positions were recorded and important pieces such as chainplates, the windlass, main hatch and skylight measured in detail. Small fragments and marks often provided vital clues in the recording process, for example, the layout of the officers' cabins in the poop.

The *Jhelum* was split into two parts by the rock causeway built across her hold and this division was used when tackling the detailed survey work. The hold forward of this was referred to as the 'fore-hold' and aft of it the 'after-hold'. The after-hold was divided into the main section of the hold and the area under the poop. The latter, which had a separate set of beams, was referred to as the 'poop-hold'. The crew's accommodation in the bow was not termed the forecastle but the crew's accommodation because the vessel was flush-decked. Most components were not lettered or numbered because their position could be fixed by reference to their position or to components joined to them, for example, the 'port hold beam clamp'.[2] The exceptions were the beams. There were four series of these: hold beams, deck beams, poop deck beams, poop hold beams. They were lettered:

1. hold beams   HA to HO
2. deck beams   DA to DV
3. poop deck beams   PA to PG
4. poop hold beams   PHA to PHC

All measurements were in feet and inches.

The fill in the hold was excavated in nine places. In January 1987, the iron stanchion under hold beam HD, fore-mast rigging and chainplates were revealed between hold beams HF and HG. In December 1987, six trenches were dug on the starboard side to take measurements from the turn of the bilge and at the ends. Finally, in February 1990, the bow and stern were re-excavated to uncover the stemson, sternson and the keelson forward, and the stanchion at hold beam B was extracted. The work was mainly directed at revealing hidden features of the hull and to fixing essential measurements. There was no stratification in the fill. The various trenches and pits revealed a variety of inorganic domestic rubbish. The latter yielded useful information about the history of the wreck after 1871. As the excavations were spaced throughout the length of the hull, it was considered that a representative sample of the fill was examined. Digging could only be carried out at low tide and was slowed down by the confined space and the jumble of material in the mud. This included wire rope, glass, timber, boulders, bricks and ironwork. It was impossible to dry out the trenches even on the lowest tides. Shoring the sides was also difficult and the excavation of the deadwood and keelson at the bow had to be carried out over several tides from 2nd to 8th February 1990. The more interesting items excavated, such as the glass bottles, were deposited at the Falklands Museum.

The wreck was photographed overall and in detail on all three field trips in 1987 and 1990. Work in progress was also recorded. So far as possible, recording was in black and white, colour print, and colour transparency. The main types of film shot were Ilford HP5, Kodak Tri-X, Kodak Vericolor 2, Kodak Gold 200 and Ektachrome 200 or 400. The main survey was carried out by Paul Browne, Senior A-V Technician at Merseyside Maritime Museum, in November and December 1987. This was on 120 roll film using a Mamiya RB67 camera. The whole wreck was photographed from the outside and inside the hold in order to produce a high-quality record of the hull structure. The underwater photography concentrated on the bow, the stern and the port side, which were clear of kelp. The work on the outside of the wreck was carried out using a tripod mounted in the work boat on calm days. In the hold, the water and an unevenness of the fill made it occasionally

The loading port area was built up with a causeway of rock topped off with a wooden deck. A large quantity of pieces of Royal Pottery Weston-Super-Mare flower pots were found in this area. The starboard port had been fitted with doors. The diagonal timbers at the top and to the left of the picture are the starboard combing and forward headledge of the main hatch. The angled timber below them is the remains of hold beam HF and behind them the main deck beam HK and the half beam HL are visible.

difficult to photograph all parts of the same level and angle. Structures such as the stern were also divided by different deck levels. Small components and features were photographed on 35mm film. More 35mm pictures were taken as field notes to assist the writing up of the detailed descriptions on return to Liverpool. Aerial pictures and video were also taken from a FIGAS plane and these were supplemented by some excellent aerial shots by Mr. R. Sampson.[3]

There were a number of earlier photographs of the wreck. A general view of the harbour looking towards the narrows taken by William Biggs in 1871 shows her at anchor off the East Jetty. Photographs of Stanley Harbour taken in 1888 by Gustav Schulz show her in her present position with the list to port and the roof.[4] John Elliott

The after-hold between hold beams HL and HM was filled with black liquid mud. Note the remains of asbestos roofing sheets which had been stored above and the long angled arms of the 'rider' knees.

of Doncaster took two excellent photographs of her in 1964. The first detailed internal survey was carried out in 1966 by Karl Kortum, the retired Director of the National Maritime Museum, San Francisco. In 1976, the late Peter Throckmorton, curator-at-large of the National Maritime Historical Society, and Hilton Matthews took another internal series, and in 1977 the Cambridge University Expedition photographed all the wrecks in the harbour for the National Maritime Museum, Greenwich. M.K. Stammers photographed the wreck in 1978 for Merseyside County Museum. These illustrate her general condition and features lost in the fire on board in 1983. A number of later photographs have been received from Nicholas Dean of the *Snowsquall* Recovery team and from Major Martin Amlôt of the 1st Battalion, the King's Regiment, who served in the Falklands in 1986. All those pictures provided useful information on the rate of deterioration.

Video recordings of the wreck, its surroundings and work on board were also made in January and November–December 1987 with Sony Camcorder and Sony D X C 3000 cameras. These tapes have been used to make a short film and extracts have been included on the multi-screen presentation on shipbuilding on Merseyside in the 'Builders of Great Ships' gallery at Merseyside Maritime Museum.

Finally, a number of samples of wood, metal, sailcloth, glass and china, together with examples of plants growing on the timbers were taken back to Liverpool for further study and display with the sanction of the Receiver of Wreck. Some of these, together with a selection of Paul Browne's fine photographs, were incorporated in a Merseyside Maritime Museum exhibition on the *Jhelum* and the other Falkland wrecks in 1989–91.

GENERAL HULL CONDITION AND LAYOUT

The hulk of the *Jhelum* lay at the upper end of Stanley harbour opposite Sulivan House on Ross Road West, 200 feet from the shore, with a list of about 20 degrees and the fore end twisted further to port. Her bow pointed towards Moody Brook and she was beached on soft sand. At low-water spring tides there was 6 feet of water at her bow and 6 feet 6 inches at her stern. A wooden jetty linked her to the shore. Her hull was substantially intact but lacked masts and deck fittings. Many fastenings were loose, corroded and weakened. But much of the timber was in good condition, especially where it was protected. Even timber that has rotted on the surface usually had a sound heart. Much of the outer planking on the port side was missing, and on the starboard side an area of 'wind and water' planking was loose or missing. The forward main deck had been stripped of its planking and its beams were missing or rotting. A loading port had been cut through both sides at the main hatch and a rock-built causeway levelled off with planking (which had broken off) connected the port and starboard openings. The upper part of the starboard fore-hold had begun to heel over at a steeper angle in recent years, while the port side had begun to spread outwards. This had been caused by a loss of structural strength, the unrelenting pressure of wind and waves and increased shipping activity since 1982. This is dealt with in more detail in Chapter 14. Windows had been cut in the tween-decks and a roof has been added to the after section. There was a large amount of rock, mud and other material in the hold. A fire in the poop in 1983 had charred the interior, destroying evidence of the original decor and fittings and burning the starboard planking.

Jim Forrester excavating the stern. He is standing on the stemson with a starboard arm of the stern crutch and pointer above this, all to his left. Note the character of the fill with wire, rigging, glass, ceramics, mud, etc.

The 1987 pre-disturbance survey of the hold identified five different areas in the hold:

1.   The fore-hold forward of the loading port causeway: mud, rock, domestic rubbish and loose timbers from the ship.
2.   The causeway, consisting of local rock with a wooden platform to level it.
3.   The port side of the after-hold; black mud and covered with water at low tide.
4.   The starboard side of the after-hold: white sand, with fewer pieces of rock and domestic rubbish than other areas. The sand near the two iron tanks was stained orange.
5.   The poop hold, below the after accommodation; a raised plateau of orange mud with a high concentration of domestic rubbish.

The hull was carvel built, with rounded entrance forward, and a hollow forefoot, straight flat floors amidships round bilge and a run aft that starts just forward of the break of the poop. There was a slight tumble home, and the bow had some flare.

Another feature of the overall design was the lack of sheer, which amounted to no more than 1 foot in her whole length. Although the hull was distorted, this has been established by measurement. It was not uncommon for ships of the mid-19th century to be built with little sheer. This can be observed in contemporary models, plans and pictures. One example is the contemporary model of the snow *Black Prince*, built at Maryport in 1838.[5] The *Jhelum* had no forecastle, and her poop deck was raised 3 feet 2 inches above the main deck. The crew's quarters were in the tween-decks at the bow and most of the hull was designed for carrying cargo, with three hatches, the two water tanks and the chain locker abaft the main mast. The officer's and ship's stores were accommodated under the raised quarter deck. This seems to have been typical of vessels of similar size and date.

Notes

1.   A note in *Lloyd's Register Survey* 27950 indicates that she had undergone an earlier survey, 19814, and was the subject of a special report in February 1866. These do not appear to have survived.
2.   The terms generally used are from the *Lloyd's Register Surveys* and Captain Paasch's *Marine Dictionary* (Antwerp, 1895).
3.   All the negatives and transparencies are incorporated in the collections of the Merseyside Maritime Museum. The 35mm ones are filed by month, year and negative number with the suffix C or BW to indicate colour or black and white. Large format negatives, which were all shot in January 1987, have the prefix F and are sequentially numbered.
4.   An album of Schulz's views of the Falklands is in the Frampton Collection, Southampton Maritime Museum.
5.   M.M.M. Collection, accession no. 57.7. See also plans drawn from model in W. Salisbury, 'Making Use of Ship Models', *Liverpool Bulletin*, Vol. XIV, pp. 11–12.

CHAPTER SEVEN

THE STRUCTURE
1: KEEL AND FRAMING

This chapter describes the main components of the *Jhelum*'s structure, at the time of the 1987 and 1990 surveys, including the keel, keelson, frames, bow and stern framing.

The keel measured 13 inches 'sided' by 14 inches 'moulded' in contemporary terminology and was made of rock elm joined by 6-foot scarphs. The above terms have been replaced by the more widely understood 'wide' and 'deep' for the rest of the description of the hull timbers. Most of it was buried but the parts at the bow and stern were accessible, though below the water. There was a false keel below it. The stern and sternposts were fastened to each end of the keel. Between the keel and the false keel there was a dovetail shaped bronze 'stopwater'. The bottom frames (floors) were fastened to the upper face of the keel and the keelsons were fitted on top of them. The keelson measured 14 inches wide by 18 inches deep and was sawn from African oak. It was excavated at the bow and probed for amidships. There were two bilge keelsons, 14 x 16 inches, made from pitch pine, but these were not found. All these components were fastened by copper bolts $1^{1}/_{4}$ inches in diameter. It was not possible to discover the position of the scarphs nor the number and position of the copper bolts.[1]

The frames were set at right angles to the keel in pairs except for the cant frames at each end. They determined the shape of the vessel. Each frame consisted of five sections: floor timber, first, second and third futtocks, and top timber. The joints in each frame of a pair were staggered to improve their overall strength. The two floor timbers were fastened together, each measuring 12 inches across by 16 inches deep, with a 3-inch space between each pair. The futtocks and the top timbers were of smaller scantling, from 12 x 10 inches at the first futtock to $8^{1}/_{2}$ x $6^{1}/_{2}$ inches at the top timber. The differences in thickness between the floor timbers and the futtocks was 2 inches and that for the top timbers was 4 inches. Each pair of frames was fastened together horizontally by iron bolts. Their height alternated up or down from one pair of frames to the next. The frame timbers were joined together either by diagonal scarphs or by triangular chocks. With the latter the two timbers had their inside faces cut diagonally, and the ends butted together. The resulting shallow triangle was filled by the chock. All three pieces were fastened together by treenails. Where the frames were not in the right position to receive the bolts of the Fell's patent knees, a filler piece had been fitted between the two frames, for example at HF. They were made of

The bow framing, with the stempost at the centre. Note the gap between the knightheads at the top for the bowsprit. The much wasted main deck breasthook is below it. This has the remains of a lodging knee on the left-hand side to fasten it to main deck beam DA. The two lighter-coloured timbers below it are modern crawling boards which rest on the hold-beam breasthook. The ceiling to left of the stempost and below this breasthook has been cut away to form a timber port. The latter was later filled in and a strengthening vertical timber added. The iron breasthook below is broken at its throat bolt as reported in the March 1871 survey.

English oak. It was difficult to be precise on the number of cant frames. They finished between hold beams HC and HD and between poop beams PB and PC at the stern. Most of the frames were intact, except where cut down at the loading ports or eroded by the sea at the wind and water level on the starboard forward side. Paired frames were an innovation in good-quality, early 19th-century ships. The method was first developed in the royal dockyards during the Napoleonic Wars. The use of horizontal iron bolts instead of chocks between the top timbers was another indication of a good-quality vessel.[2]

The main components of the bow framing were the stempiece, apron and deadwood. The stempiece measured $11^{1}/_{2}$ x $19^{3}/_{4}$ inches. The upper part was smaller, with a long tapering scarph which started level with the top of the wooden sheathing on the starboard side. It was not clear how they were fastened together but there was a single through-fastened copper bolt to the back of the apron visible above the iron breasthook. The apron, 8 x $16^{1}/_{2}$ inches, was fastened by iron bolts above the waterline. The stem knee or stemson, $8^{1}/_{2}$ x $12^{1}/_{2}$ inches, a heavy wooden bracket behind the apron, anchored the bow to the top of the keelson. The top face of the stemson had a shallow mortise cut into it. The apron had the rabbet for the hull planking cut into it. Five breasthooks were mentioned in the *Lloyd's Survey*. Only four were found. The lower two were made of iron, $3^{1}/_{4}$ x $1^{3}/_{4}$ inches. The upper one was broken through at the apron bolt.[3] The two main breasthooks were large pieces of crooked oak about 12 inches deep and fixed with iron bolts at the level of the main and hold deck beams. The hold beam breasthook did not

Starboard bow, the individual components of the bow are clearly visible, along with the hawse hole and cathead. The opening for the later WC is below the cathead and two of the steel fixing plates for the wire ropes tying the two sides of the bow together are on either side of this. There is a section of diagonally fixed wooden sheathing below it.

have the precise shape to fit the bow, and there were chocks to provide a snug fit with the apron and knightheads. Lodging knees at each end of the breasthook linked it with the first hold beam HA. Long iron through-bolts fastened all three components. On the starboard side, there was a wedge-shaped chock between the main deck beam DA and the knee at the end of the breasthook. Both the top surfaces of these two breasthooks were rotted badly and the long iron bolts which fastened them to the apron, the knightheads and hawse pieces were exposed. There was a small horizontal timber above the main deck level near the top of the apron. It was of much smaller section (about 4 inches deep) than the two breasthooks. The aft face had rotted away, leaving iron bolts projecting and it was fastened to the hawsepieces, knightheads and apron. There were three semi-circles cut out of its forward face.

An iron strap linked the top of the port knightheads and the three hawse-pieces. The knightheads and the three hawsepieces per side were through fastened to the apron at its top and at the hold beam breasthook. At their lower ends they tapered to butt up to the first cant frame. They were fastened to the hull planking by treenails. The three hawse holes with their cast iron pipes had been fitted through the hawse timbers. On the outside the hawse pipes were flanged to protect the timbers from the anchor cables and on the inside the lower halves projected beyond the timbers to protect them from the cables. In 1966, there was also a cast iron flange on the starboard inside. There were two to port, 7 inches and 9 inches in diameter, and one to starboard, 9 inches in diameter. The holes in the timbers through which the pipes passed were lined with lead sheet. On the port side, all of the above timbers had part of their bottom ends cut away to form a timber port, measuring 32 x 33 inches. This was later planked over and a new short framing timber had been fitted to bridge the gap. It was presumed that this was cut for loading mahogany logs at Tupilco on voyages 16 and 17.

The angle of the port bow was caused by the collapse of the deck beams of the bow. Note the features of the starboard rail and cathead and the wooden lodging knees which go aft as far as main deck beam DC. This also represents the length of the crew accommodation. The two wooden knees with their mouldings and the iron knee of the bow are clearly visible and indicate the almost vertical position of the female bust figurehead.

On the outer forward face of the bow there was a complex arrangement of protective and shape-giving timbers. The forefoot was missing, but above this the cut-water
or 'independent piece' was still in position, butted up to the forefoot. The knee of the
head, the bracket, projecting in front of the stempiece, fitted on top of the cutwater. It
was made up of the outer bobstay-piece with four filling chocks between it and the
stempiece. The horizontal lace-piece was clamped over the filling chocks. A pair of
diagonal iron bolts fastened these to the stem and a vertical iron bolt ran through to
the bobstay-piece. At the outer end of the knee of the head a surviving diagonal bolt
would have secured the missing figurehead. The knee of the head was braced by an
angled iron lodging knee and two cheekpieces, wooden lodging knees, above it. The
outer faces of the cheekpieces had decorative mouldings. Their outer ends are angled
upwards and extended to the base of the figurehead. These were in excellent condition on the port side. The head rails were above the cheekpieces and were missing.
Three of their supporting brackets survived on the port and two on the starboard. The
cast iron hawsepipes passed through the horizontal timbers bolted on the outside of
planking. On the port side of the stempiece, there was a small triangular timber to fill
the gap between the stem and the knighthead. Close by was a line of copper nails and
a fragment of lead which suggested that the top of the stem was sheathed. The bow
framing was built in a heavy timber to resist the impact of being driven into seas, and
to take the stresses of riding at anchor and the pressures of the head sails set on the
bowsprit. The broken breasthook was damaged before the *Jhelum*'s arrival at Stanley in
1870, and it would be interesting to discover the cause. Perhaps it was as a result of
her collision at Rosario in January of that year. The figurehead was a female bust

Lower stern framing in the hold. The
sternpost at the centre is flanked by two
short frames with the transom timbers
above. The fashion timbers lie either
side of these and they tied into the transom and the ceiling and frames by the
iron pointers. The wing transom lies at
the top behind the timbers supporting
the poop planking.

The view of the upper transom shows the rider transom with a heavy knee at each end to act as a joint with the outer horn timbers. It also shows the horn timbers which frame the counter (transom), the sternpost with the rudder trunk abaft. The hatch to the hold is in front of it and two deck planks have been removed to permit measuring. At the top centre, some charred panelling and the skylight opening are visible.

according to the *Liverpool Shipping Register* and the cheekpieces show that it would have been in an upright position. The construction of the knee on the head was typical of the mid-19th century.[4]

The stern framing was intact and its main components were the sternpost and transom beam or wing transom. All other components depended on these. The sternpost measured $9^3/4$ x 12 inches, reduced to $6^1/4$ inches above the transom beam and was fashioned from an unknown species of African hardwood. It was joined to the keel, and to the keelson, by the stern knee or sternson, $10^1/2$ x $14^1/2$ inches, on its forward side. There were two short cant frames on either side of the sternpost and forward of these were the fashion timbers, 10 x $6^1/2$ inches, fixed at right angles to the keelson. They framed the outer sides of the transom. They were made of two main timbers because of their compound curve and were scarphed approximately 6 feet up from the deadwood. There was a smaller timber joined to the upper end of each upper main timber where they projected into the poop accommodation. This latter was fastened with five treenails on the starboard side, two of which overlapped. Six transoms or transom timbers of crooked timber filled the triangle between the fashion timbers and the transom beam. There were shallow mortises cut in the fore side of the sternpost to receive them. The first transom lay on top of the stern knee and was fastened by two treenails to the sternpost, with another fixing it to the outer planking. The second had 1 copper bolt and 1 treenail to the sternpost and 5 treenails, 2 to port and 3 to starboard, for the planking. The remaining 4 had single copper bolts to the sternpost and the following treenails for the outer planking: 3rd – 1 treenail to sternpost, 4 to port, 2 to starboard; 4th – 4 to port, 2 to starboard; 5th – 4 to port, 7 to starboard; 6th – 8 to port, 8 to starboard. The 5th and 6th transoms also had copper bolts for fastening the pointers.

The whole lower stern structure was tied together and to the ceiling and frames forward of the fashion timbers by 2 iron pointers, $3^{1}/_{2}$ x $1^{1}/_{4}$ inches. Their tops were fastened into the forward face of the wing transom and they were fixed by 10 copper bolts along their length. An iron crutch or breasthook was fastened at its throat to the deadwood and ran diagonally upwards and forwards.

The transom timber carried the framing of the counter, the upper part of the stern. It was fastened to the sternpost by 2 iron bolts. On its foreside there were 4 timbers in line which supported the ends of the poop accommodation deck planking. The 2 outer pieces were fastened to the fashion timbers and butted to the others, except for a rough scarph on the starboard side. There was a rider transom fastened on top of it by 10 iron bolts and a large knee is scarphed to it either end to form a bracket to fasten it to the horn timbers, and the top of the fashion timbers. These knees were angled at 45° to the accommodation deck. On their forward face they had 4 iron bolts through to the counter planking and 2 small treenails. The starboard knee had 2 holes bored

The port-side junction of the ceiling and the fashion timber is in the right-hand corner. To the left of the curving fashion timber is the wing transom with the knee above it which fastens it to the outer horn timber. Note the treenails and the triangular chock on the knee where it is butted up to the horn timber.

Poop deck, starboard quarter, with sawn-down horn timbers and the deck planking mortised to receive the archboard. The upright timber on the right was a later addition for carrying the corrugated iron sheeting.

for treenails, which do not seem to have been used. Another iron bolt was driven upwards to fasten the heel of the second horn timber. The knees' upper faces had single iron bolts which fastened them to the after side of the fashion timber. Both knees had triangular chocks fitted on their outer sides. The starboard chock was larger than that on the port side.

There were 14 horn (stern) timbers. The longer ones had their heels fastened to the rider transom. The outer horn timber $12^1/_4$ x $10^1/_2$ inches was butted up to the fashion timber. There appeared to be no fastening between them. The ends of the poop side planking were tree-nailed to its outer face. There were 3 vertical timbers on the forward face whose tops went up to the poop deck waterway. These provided more fixing places for the poop side planking. The top of the outer horn timber was mortised into the poop deck beam PG. The second horn timber was butted up to the top of the large knee and was angled towards the outer horn timber. At its top there was a chock between it and the outer horn timber where they emerged on the poop deck. The horn timbers have been cut off 6 inches above deck level. They would have continued upwards and outwards and been mortised into the taff rail to form the stern rail of the poop. The sternpost horn timbers were knotched to fit on either side of the rudder trunk, and they too originally projected through to the poop deck above. There were 4 timbers to either side of the stern-post timbers that were alternately long and short. The long timbers also went through to the poop deck. The short ones allowed space for 4 stern windows to light the main saloon.

This stern view shows the upper line of the wooden sheathing to port and starboard of the sternpost with some of the diagonal boards still in place. To port a small section of the moulding of the stern decoration is visible while above John Kearon's head is the burnt piece of the back-board for the stern carving. Note the four stern windows which lit the saloon and the two after cabins. The aperture near the moulding is a later modification.

Sternpost, rudder trunk and gudgeons from below. Note the construction of the trunk.

The top of the stern post with rudder gudgeon and the rudder trunk. Note the original poop deck planking.

Starboard side of the stern post with three surviving depth lead marks. To the left of the '6' and '7' there is a surviving length of metal sheathing. There are also many sheathing nails, e.g., lower right-hand corner and holes of sheathing nails visible. The diagonal timber projecting from the '6' upwards marked the upper limit of the wooden sheathing.

The 14 counter planks had various lengths to allow for the sternpost, rudder trunk and stern windows and were spiked to the horn timbers, with one iron spike per plank per horn timber. The upper ones were missing or charred. A 12 x 12 inch hole has been cut on the port side. Its purpose was not established. The outer face of the sternpost carried the rudder gudgeons. The lowest was of bronze and was still in position fastened by 2 bolts. The uppermost is an iron forging $2^1/2$ x $^1/2$ inches which was shrunk on to the top of the sternpost, which in turn was rebated to fit it. The diameter of the hole for the rudder pintle was $2^3/4$ inches. A similar iron gudgeon was fitted at the bottom of the rudder trunk and a fourth (bronze) fitting was missing. Its position was fixed by the shallow mortise cut into the outer face of the sternpost. This had its top level with the top of the yellow metal sheathing. The rudder trunk was built through the counter on the outer face of the sternpost. It consisted of 12 timbers, forming three sides. The outer side is semi-circular and those to port and starboard were angled at 45° to the sides of the sternpost. The timbers were rebated on their edges and joined by the insertion of slips of timber. They were nailed to the deck planking at the top. On the starboard side of the sternpost there were 3 lead draught marks, '6', '7' and '8', with an '8' only on the port side.

The stern framing was complicated because it extended the upper hull beyond the sternpost to provide 'lift' aft, and to give a steering platform and additional accommodation. Its design can be traced back to 18th-century ships. For example, a similar design was illustrated by Falconer in 1780 for a small warship.[5] It was also similar to that of the *Actaeon*, built in Miramichi, New Brunswick, in 1838, which lies at the West Jetty at Stanley. Unlike some early 19th-century ships of similar size the *Jhelum* did not have quarter galleries or even dummy ones, such as those on the stern of a ship photographed in dry dock at Swansea in 1846 by the Rev. Calvert Jones.[6] In 1987, the counter planking above the starboard stern windows had a timber with a curved end nailed to it. This has since dropped off. This was probably the backboard for the stern decoration. One could guess that this would have been a simple carved form such as cable laid ropework. This would have been typical for a ship of the *Jhelum*'s date and size. There were also lines of simple mouldings below the stern windows. A short fragment was still fixed on the port side. The decoration and window frames would have been picked out in white (or possibly gold leaf) with the ship's name and home port painted at the bottom of the transom.[7]

Notes

1. The dimensions quoted throughout this and chapter 9 are from *Lloyd's Register Survey* no. 18262 and survey measurements.
2. B. Greenhill, with S. Manning, *The Evolution of the Wooden Ship* (London, 1988), pp. 112–15, 118.
3. The survey conducted by the officers of HMS *Galatea* in 1871, see Chapter 5 and Appendix 6, reported that this was broken and that there was a higher iron breasthook which is missing.
4. See paintings of the barque *Amity* of about 1840, accession no. 1964.194.1 and the ship *Princess Charlotte* of 1815, accession no. 1970.246.5 show how the shape of the head changed in the early 19th century. The *Amity*, which is similar to the *Jhelum*, was simplified with less elaborate rails and an upright bust instead of an angled full-length figurehead, Merseyside Maritime Museum.
5. W. Falconer, *An Universal Dictionary of the Marine* (London, 1780), plate XII.
6. R. Buckman, *The Photographic Work of Calvert Richard Jones* (London, 1990), plate 19.
7. See for example model of ship *Rienzi* (1851), accession no. 36.10.6, M.M.M.

CHAPTER EIGHT

THE STRUCTURE 2: LONGITUDINALS AND DECK BEAMS

LONGITUDINALS

The hold and the deck beams of the *Jhelum* were supported by two continuous longit-udinal timbers, the shelf with the clamp below them. The hold beams had two more longitudinals above them – the waterway with the spirketting above it. The deck beams had just a waterway on the main deck which was butted up to the covering board. The poop hold and deck beams had their own shelves. There was a short bilge stringer in the bow which was not the same as the bilge keelsons mentioned in the *Lloyd's Survey*.

The hold beam shelf, $10^3/_4$ x $6^1/_2$ inches, began at the bow at the leading cant frame and ran aft as far as the sternward end of the lodging knee of hold beam HO. It was fastened to the frames by $1^1/_4$-inch iron bolts and treenails. These were stag-gered with one of each per frame. Additional iron bolts had been added, probably as repairs. The lower edge had a moulding cut into it. It was scarphed with hook scarphs at hold beams HE and HJ on either side. The hold beam clamp, 9 x $4^1/_2$ inches, was fastened immediately below the hold beam shelf; it started from the first cant frame and ran aft beyond the clamp. It was tapered to a point at its aft end, which terminated under poop hold beam PHB. It was fastened by $1^1/_4$-inch bolts at its top edge and treenails below which were found approximately at every fifth frame. It was not a continuous timber but its several sections were butted up to one another.

The main deck beam shelf, $10^1/_4$ x 5 inches ran from the bow right through to the outer horn timber. It was fastened in a similar way to the hold beam shelf, and was scarphed at deck beams DE and DN. The port side section from the bow to DD was in poor condition and missing at the loading port. The main deck clamp, 9 x $4^1/_2$ inches, ran from the bow to the horn timber and was intersected by the top of the fashion timber. Fastenings were similar to the hold beam clamp, and the port side was butted between deck beams DI and DJ, and DD and DQ on the port side. On the

Starboard tween deck, 1966. Note the planking of the crew accommodation and the remains of its bulk-head to right of centre. The mortises for carlings for the foremast are visible on the extreme left. The deck beams in the foreground have spikes in them from the timber walkway to the WC cut through the starboard side.

starboard side, the butts were between DI and DJ and DQ and DR. The forward end of the port side clamp was made from two pieces of timber from deck beam DA to DD. These timbers were bolted together by 3/4-inch bolts at 24 1/2-inch centres. A heavier bolt had been driven through a six-sided chock between DF and DD. This and the two-piece clamp were probably repairs. It should be noted that the Lloyd's surveyor crossed out the words 'shelf pieces' and referred to the above mentioned timbers as clamps. They were made of African oak and Australian hardwood.

The hold beam waterways, 9 3/4 x 5 3/4 inches, lay on top of the hold beams with the spirketting above. As with the shelves and clamps, it was noted that the surveyor

crossed out the word spirketting. However, Paasch's Dictionary used this term for
the thicker strake of the ceiling above the waterway and such a strake was observed
on the *Jhelum*. The hold-beam waterways ran from the bow at the first cant frames
through to the forward face of the fashion timbers. On the port side, it was missing
from bow to hold beam HD and at the loading port. It had a moulding on its top
edge and was fastened by one iron bolt per frame. These were staggered on alternate frames. They were scarphed in three places below main deck beams DC, DG
and DL, and were made of pitch pine or a similar type of pine. The spirketting for
the hold beams, 9³/₄ x 3¹/₂ inches, ran from the bow (first cant frame) to the forward face of the fashion timber and on the port side it was missing as far as the after
end of the loading port except for a short length between hold beams HC and HE.
It too was made of the same type of pine. It was in three pieces, butted between
DD and DE, at DH and under PHC.

   The main deck waterway, 8 x 7 inches, ran from the bow through the break of
poop into poop accommodation to just aft of the end of the lodging knee of main
deck beam DV. Most of it had been stripped off or rotted right through the fore-hold.
A short section survived at the starboard bow and near main deck beam DM. These
and other sections observed under the corrugated roof were in poor condition. There
was a smaller section waterway across the break of the poop. This was a quarter round
in section and was observed under the roof but could not be measured.

The after-hold 'tween deck' from the starboard side of the loading port. The two cast-iron deck beam
stanchions to the left stand on either side of the after-hatch the carlings of which are just visible. Beyond
them lies the deck of the poop accommodation. The corroded top of the starboard water tank is in the
foreground.

The poop hold and deck beams had shelves and no clamps. There was no waterway on the accommodation deck. The poop deck proper had a covering board and no waterway. The poop hold beam shelf, 5^1/$_4$ x 2 inches, started at the break of the poop from the iron hanging knee of main deck beam DV to under the aft end of poop hold beam PHC. At this point, it had tapered down to 1-inch thickness. All the poop hold beams sat in shallow mortises. The shelf was fastened into alternate frames by two staggered treenails and one per intermediate frame. Both port and starboard were intact and in good condition. The poop deck beam shelf, 7^1/$_4$ x 3 inches, ran from the forward end of poop deck beam PA aft to PG where it ended on the forward face of the outer horn timber. It had a shallow mortise cut in to fit poop deck beam PF. Both sides were intact and in good condition.

DECK BEAMS

The deck beams of the *Jhelum* were fitted at four different levels: hold, poop hold (below the accommodation), main deck and poop. There were 15 hold, 3 poop hold, 22 main deck and 7 poop deck beams. Three of the main deck beams – DE, DL and DM – were half beams. All were sawn from either English or African oak. The impression, based on those in good condition in the after section, was that most were of the latter wood. Main deck beams, DA, DC, DE, DG, DJ, DL, DM, DP and DT did not have hold beams below them. Main deck beams were all cambered on both top and bottom faces. The lower edges had moulding cut into them. All the beams in the fore-hold were in poor condition. DA, DB, DC, DD, DE, DK, DL and DM were incomplete or missing. DG, DH, DI and DJ, though intact, were weak. DN and beams aft of it under the roof were in good condition except for some rot in the port side of DN and DO. DS had a 4-foot section sawn out of it on the starboard side. DV and PA above it had been cut through their centres to create access from the hold to the poop. Only HC was intact in the fore-hold. The centre section of HF, which had collapsed into the fore-hold, had two iron plates bolted fore and aft. This must have been a repair, and reflected the lack of strength around the main hatch noted in the HMS *Galatea* survey. Hold beams aft of HI were intact and in sound condition except for the port side top faces of HI and HJ, which had rotted. The poop hold beams and the deck beams were intact except PE, which had been cut away under the skylight. PD and PF were rotted and weak. The average dimensions of the main deck beams was 9 x 8^3/$_4$ inches. The largest, DA and DH, were 11 inches wide and the smallest, DE, DM and DT, 6^1/$_2$ inches. The hold beams were larger, averaging 11 x 11 inches, and had less variations in size. The poop hold beams were 9^1/$_2$ x 7 inches and the poop deck beams 7^1/$_2$ x 6 inches on average.

There were 26 cast-iron centre stanchions, 2^3/$_8$ inches in diameter. The lower 15 were fixed between the top of the keelson and the bottom face of the hold beams. The upper ones were fitted between the top face of the hold beams and the bottom face of the main deck beams. They had flanges at either end with two holes and were

Close-up of the main deck version of Fell's patent knee, on main deck beam DP. The lower arm is bolted into the shelf. Note the moulding on the deck beam.

fastened by iron bolts. Stanchions DI–HC and DF–HD were dug up for measuring and to check the sheer. HI had a 7-inch deep packing piece of timber on its bottom face so that the stanchion could be fitted. There seemed to be no reason why this packing piece had been fitted unless the yard had exhausted the stock of the longer ones. It was of the same pattern as the others and therefore not a later repair.

The hold beams had their ends supported on the shelves and clamps, and were fixed to these longitudinal timbers by horizontal lodging knees. There was only one pair of wooden hanging knees which were fitted to PA at the break of the poop. Wooden lodging knees were used at the ends of the ship and Fell's patent iron knees where the two sides were parallel. All the wooden knees were fastened by iron bolts to the frames and beams: 3 to the long arm, 2 to the short and 1 at the throat. The Fell's patent knees for the hold beams consisted of a pair of forged wrought iron T-shaped brackets bolted together by three iron bolts. Each arm of the T changed from a flat section to a circular one, with the hole in the centre to take a threaded bolt from the beam shelf at the bottom and the waterway at the top. The main deck beam version was similar but L-shaped and was only bolted to the shelf.

The iron hanging knees supported the main deck beams and were fastened by four iron bolts through the ceiling, shelf and clamp to the frames. The short arm had three iron bolts to attach it to the bottom face of its deck beam. They were shaped to fit the shelf and waterway. The port knee of DC was angled forward and the starboard aft. Deck beam DQ had a distinct bend in it and its starboard knee was also angled forward to ensure it landed on a frame. It was stamped 'S VIII' on its short arm. DS and DU's knees were also forged to fit their particular position. The hold beams had knee riders which were hanging knees with extended, angled arms. Those forward of the loading port were angled forward about 60° and those aft were angled aft at the same angles. They were fastened to the frames and ceiling by six copper bolts and three iron bolts to the beam. Occasionally the top-most bolt of the long arm was an iron one.

The poop hold beams had no hanging knees. Their lodging knees were all wooden ones. The poop deck beams PA and PB had wooden lodging knees and they also appeared between PF and PG. Between PC and PF iron staple knees had been fitted. They were fastened to filling pieces between the beams and the frames behind them by four threaded iron bolts. They were attached to each beam by three iron bolts.

Both wood and iron knees were in good condition under the roof. But where they were exposed the long arms of the rider knees between HC and HG in the forward hold were delaminating and a heavy crust of iron oxides had formed on their surfaces. The hanging knee from the port side of DD had been removed and was lying loose in the hold until taken for safekeeping at the Falklands Museums in 1987.[1] The Fell's knees were in good condition under the roof except for the port side of DN, which was rusted through on its forward end. Port DD and starboard HH are missing. In general, the iron knees protected by the roof and above the tide line were in good condition and have traces of coating of red lead covered with black paint, or tar.

Hanging knees were forged to fit their particular deck beams. This shows the starboard one of main deck beam DQ which has been cranked forward. Note the mouldings on the clamp and shelf of the main deck beam, the waterway and spirketting of the hold beam and round the air courses.

The wooden lodging knees between main deck beams DV (left) and DU (right) at the break of the poop. Note the cranked-iron hanging knee. The wooden lodging knee below fastens the first poop hold beam PHA to the frames.

The carlings or carlins were longitudinal timbers that connected the deck beams fore and aft. They framed openings in the deck for hatches and masts. From the bow, the windlass was carried on two, connecting DA and DB. The foremast carlings were between DD and DF, with half-beam DE at their centre. They have disappeared but their position could be traced by the two mortises cut in the forward face of DF and the two mortises immediately below on the aft face of HC. The mortises on HC are 12 x 5 inches to port and $9^3/8$ x 5 inches to starboard and $1^1/2$ inches deep. The port one still had an iron bolt through its centre. The inner edges of the mortises were 27 inches apart. The main hatch carlings were between DK and DN. Half beams HL and HM were fastened into them. HH, judging by the large cross section of the surviving stump on the port side, would have gone right across, and there would have been carlings between it, HG and HI. The main-mast carlings were immediately aft of the main hatch between DN and DO. The starboard one survived and measured 8 x $6^1/2$ inches. It was jointed to the underside of the deck beam by a halved joint. There was a shallow mortise to receive it on the forward face of DO, where it was fixed by an iron bolt. The fore end of this carling had been cut away. There was a filler piece above it, 4 inches deep, to level it off with the top of the beam. The said carling had mortises, 3 inches at each end of the inside (port) face to fit the mast partners, which were missing. The distance between its inside (port face) and the inside face of the mortise for the missing port carling was $24^1/2$ inches, which gave an approximate diameter for the mast. The after hatch carlings, 5 x $6^1/2$ inches, were between DR and

DS. They were mortised into the upper part of the aft and forward faces of their two deck beams. The distance between their inside faces was 4 feet 6 inches. The mizzen mast carlings were missing but their mortises survive on HN and HO, and on DU and DV. The mortises measured 7 x 4 inches and $1^{1}/_{4}$ inches deep and the distance between them was $24^{1}/_{2}$ inches. Two carlings survived between PA and PB, which were above those between HN–HO and DU–DV. The distance between the latter was 6 feet 8 inches. There was a partner on the forward side of PB joining the two carlings. There were two mortises in the top face of carlings forward of the partner at PB. The after of the two mortises would have been for the forward partner of the mizzen mast. There were carlings between PC and PD (3 x 4 inches) $54^{1}/_{4}$ inches apart with a partner 3 x 6 inches on the forward face of PD for the accommodation companionway. Between PD, PE and PF, there were carlings 3 x 5 inches in two pieces. There were partners at $25^{1}/_{2}$ inches from the forward side of PE and 28 inches from its aft side in 1978 that were missing in 1987. These were all designed to support the skylight of the saloon. At the break of the poop, PA and DU were tied together by four diagonal braces ($4^{1}/_{4}$ x $2^{3}/_{4}$ inches) and four wooden stanchions ($5^{3}/_{8}$ x $5^{3}/_{8}$ inches). The bottoms of the braces were fastened with iron bolts to a small rider beam on top of DU, and the tops were fixed to the bottom face of PA. Originally there would have been two more of these braces at the centre. These must have been cut

An overall view of the 'half deck' shows the diagonal bracing and wooden hanging knees at the break of the poop. The centre section and main deck beam DV were cut away to create access from the tween and main decks. A central pair of diagonal braces were removed as well. The two heavy stanchions on either side of the 'half deck' projected through the poop deck and were probably mooring bitts. At the top left the opening for the companionway is clearly visible.

The port corner of the break of the poop with wooden knees and diagonal braces. The vertical post was a rail stanchion for the poop deck.

away when the ship was hulked. Two carlings were lying detached in the fore-hold. The first, $76^1/2$ x $12^1/2$ x 5 inches, lay underneath the port side of the windlass. It is of similar design to the surviving mainmast carling but with a mortise, 23 x 6 inches, cut in its centre. The distance between the two end joints was $57^1/2$ inches and this suggests it was fitted between DB and DC. The second lay in the starboard side of the forehold and measured 73 x $11^3/4$ x $5^1/2$ inches and had the same distance between the end joints ($57^1/2$ inches) with a mortise 19 x 6 inches.

Although the *Jhelum* had been strongly built, the survey carried out by the officers of HMS *Galatea* on 2nd March 1871 hinted at structural weakness: 'the iron stanchions fore and aft in the hold are bent and started and appear too weak for their work which has caused the upper deck to sink in the waist and under the poop . . . The main hatchway upper deck beams are broken and require replacing'. In addition, there were the iron straps on hold beam HF that were evidence of an earlier undated repair. This all suggests that the ironwork, although it saved space and was a substitute for scarce and expensive crooked timber, may have been too light in scantling. Use of iron for knees and stanchions was commonplace by 1849. Its introduction began to take place at the end of the 18th century and was advanced by Sir Robert Seppings, Surveyor to the Royal Navy, 1813–32. In Sepping's period of office, forked and T-shaped iron knees were used on naval vessels. Examples of the former can still be seen on HMS *Unicorn* (1824) at Dundee. Fell's patent knee was patented by Jonathan Fell of Workington in 1839.[2] Fell was manager of William Peile, Scott & Co's shipyard and later the Workington and Harrington Shipbuilding Co and was a shipowner too. D.R. MacGregor believes he was an innovator in fast sailing ship design who influenced other shipbuilders in the North West of England.[3] His patent specified cast-iron sidepieces unlike those of the *Jhelum*. They were also of a different layout although they acted in the same way. Whether the *Jhelum*'s knees were an improved version or a variation developed by Steel is unknown. But the *Lloyd's Register* surveyor of 1863 clearly stated that they were Fell's patent, and this was repeated on the report on Steel's *Zillah* of 1847. On the report on the *Helen Wallace* of 1848 they were termed 'double lugged T. pieces.'

Although evidence for the mast and hatch carlings was found for all three masts and two hatches, the forward deck beams were so badly wasted that no trace of a companionway to the crew's quarters nor a forehatch was found. The *Jhelum* is likely to have had both these fittings. The position of the latter will be discussed in Chapter 11.

Notes

1.   This and an example of the Fell's knee were generously given to Merseyside Maritime Museum and are due for delivery to Liverpool by the brigantine *Soren Larsen* in August 1992.
2.   Patent no. 8156, 5th August 1839. It seems to have been taken up quite widely or this seems to be implied by the *Lloyd's Register* 'Visitation Committee' report on the Workington yard in 1855 man aged by Fell who they described as 'Mr. Jonathon Fell', *the patentee* of the screw binding for beams', quoted in D.R. MacGregor, *Merchant Sailing Ships 1850–75* (London, 1984), p. 36.
3.   D.R. MacGregor, *Fast Sailing Ships* (London, 1988, 2nd edn), pp. 126–9, 201–2.

CHAPTER NINE

PLANKING AND DECK FITTINGS

PLANKING

The *Jhelum* had two 'skins'. The first was the outer hull and deck planking, the second was the ceiling which with the longitudinal strength-giving timbers (clamps, shelves etc) lined the inside of the frames. Evidence of the fittings and rig were attached to her rails and decks. There were 49 strakes of external hull planking with the following thicknesses: garboards, $3^{1}/_{2}$ inches; garboard to bilge, $3^{1}/_{2}$ inches; bilge strakes, 5 inches; bilge to wales, $3^{1}/_{2}$ inches; wales, 5 inches; topsides, 3 inches; sheerstrakes, 4 inches.

The butts of the planks were staggered so that there were three planks between butts which were also kept at least 5 feet apart. The hood ends of the planking were fastened into the rabbet at the stem and stern, and at their butts by copper 'dumps'. The main method of fastening was by treenails up to the wales. The engine-turned treenails were held tight by three wedges set in a triangle. There were two per plank per frame which were staggered. The topsides were iron-fastened. There was some evidence of repairs to the planking, with short lengths or pieces let into the main run of the planking. For example, these could be seen on the port bow, on the port side near the foremost chainplates at water level and under the third of the starboard foremast chainplates. The starboard planking was intact from the topsides down to the upper limit of the wind and water zone. But many fastenings were loose. There was about 50 feet of timber missing on the wind and waterline strake. Forward of the loading port another seven strakes above this were also missing. On the port, most of the topsides were missing from DB aft to the break of the poop. The planking of the poop was poor on both sides; the starboard side was fire-damaged and the port decaying and rotten and most of the caulking was missing.

The lower part of the hull had been sheathed in yellow metal according to the *Lloyd's Survey* and there were traces of this left at the bow and stern. Where it had been stripped off its position and the size of the sheets could be traced by the lines of coppering nails or their holes. The sheets were 24 x 7 inches on average. Above the metal sheathing there was an 18-inch band of wooden sheathing. The $6^{3}/_{4}$ x 1 inch pine boards were nailed diagonally at the stern and horizontally and diagonally at the

Starboard planking detail; the line of nails marks the upper level of the sheathing. The triangular wedging of the treenails is clearly shown.

bow. They were topped off by a half-round piece of hardwood treenailed to the planking. Sections of this sheathing survived on either side of the bow, with a large section of seven boards on the port side of the stern. Finally each run of planking up to the wales had a copper bolt with a rove fastened through to the ceiling. They appeared to be spaced at random.

The ceiling along with the longitudinal timbers described in Chapter 8 formed the inner skin of the ship. There were 27 strakes of 3-inch thick hackmatack planking in the hold plus a thicker limber strake, and bilge strake.[1] They were not caulked and there was an air course at the top of these. There were 4 widths, $2^1/2$ inches thick above the hold beam spirketting in the tween-deck with an air course between the second and the third strakes. The air course was $7^3/4$ inches deep, with a moulding and rounded ends. The air course on the starboard ran between DA–DC, DC–DF, DF–DK, DK–DO with the section at the loading port missing, DO–DQ, DQ–DS and DS–DV. To port it was missing in the fore-hold and aft ran between DN–DQ, DQ–DS and DS–DU. The air course was interrupted by the hanging knees of the main deck beams. The lower air course below the hold beams was continuous. The gaps between the hold beams had not been filled and they formed another air course. The purpose of the air courses was to let air to the frames in an attempt to deter rot. The gaps between the main deck beams had filling timbers. The ceiling was fastened chiefly by treenails below the hold beams and a combination of treenails and iron spikes above. In the starboard fore-hold there were a small number of copper bolts or dumps, for example, the two under DB in the end of one plank. Much of the ceiling

Remains of the main deck planking on the starboard side, just aft of the loading port. On the right
there are the remains of the waterway. In the centre, there is a lead patch which is perhaps a relic of
the last stormy passage.

was below the level of the hold fill. Eight strakes had been washed off at the wind and
water or 'splash zone' level on the starboard side of the fore-hold. Many strakes, especially from the beginning of the starboard run aft, had worn or were missing fastenings. The poop had a separate ceiling, 2 inches thick. There was a $2^{1}/_{2}$-inch deep air
space below the poop deck beam shelf. Most of it had been filled on the port side, but
not on the starboard. There were five strakes below the air space, then the main deck
clamp and shelf and another two strakes to deck level. The lowest rested on the poop
hold beams. The starboard side poop ceiling was badly charred and burnt through in
two places between PB and PC.

    The main deck planking, 3 x 6 inches, was yellow pine and ran from the bow to
DV. This was aft of the break of the poop, with the final length forming a platform
inside the poop accommodation. The planking had been stripped off as far back as
DN except for one section on the starboard between DM and DN. The latter had an
interesting lead patch which was perhaps a temporary repair on the last voyage. The
iron spikes survived in the tops of the deck beams. Much of the planking survived
under the roof. It was in very poor condition between DN and DP. The poop deck
planking, $2^{1}/_{2}$ x 4 inches, was exposed at the starboard break of the poop in January
1987 and at the stern in January 1990. Where exposed it was in good condition
except around the skylight and was covered in a layer of pitch. The caulking and
pitching between the seams had survived. It was fastened by one iron spike per deck
beam. The spike heads were covered by diamond-shaped wooden plugs set in pitch.
The after ends of the planks butted up to the fore side of horn timbers and projected

beyond them in the intervening spaces. Their top edge had been halved to fit the archboard, which was missing. There was evidence of wear in the poop planking, and one plank had a new section next to the stern scarphed with a V-shaped scarph. The covering board, 6 x 17 inches, ran from the hawse piece at the bow to the break of the poop. The poop deck covering board, 4 x 12 inches, ran from the break of the poop to the outer horn timber. The rail stanchions were mortised through it. On the port side it was missing from the bow to DE and at the loading port. The portion that survived was in poor condition. The starboard side covering board ran through to the loading port but it too was in poor condition. It was scarphed at the 1st, 2nd and 7th rail stanchions on the starboard side. It had survived both to port and starboard under the roof, but its condition is unknown except at port side from DN to DQ, where it had rotted badly. There were three 2-inch diameter copper scupper pipes which passed diagonally through the covering board; one either side at DP and another on the port side next to the break of the poop. Finally there was a hole for another copper scupper pipe near the starboard foremast chainplates.

DECK FITTINGS

The rails only survived forward of the loading port but were not in good condition, especially on the starboard side. They appear to have been intact except for the bulwark planking until about 1920 and were still fairly sound in the early 1960s. The rail itself, 3 x 17 inches approximately, ran between starboard stanchions 1 to 9 and port 2 to 6. The junction with the hawsepieces had been lost by 1978. The rail was scarphed at the 3rd starboard stanchion where it turned sharply into the bow. Its inside face had a moulding. The pin rail, 2 x 5 inches, for the foremast running rigging was still attached to the port rail. This had seventeen holes for belaying pins and a brass rubbing strip on its edge. A section of the starboard rail was loose and had been removed to the roofed stern section for safekeeping. There were also holes cut through the rail for the foremast chainplates. Two lengths of bulwark planking were still fixed from stanchions 4 to 10 to starboard. The poop stanchions had all been cut down, but they could be traced under the roof. On the starboard side of the poop there were 2 stanchions $4^3/_4$ x 5 inches and 4 x 4 inches, 6 inches apart; and 2 more, $4^1/_4$ x $5^1/_4$ inches and 4 x $4^3/_4$ inches and these are $47^3/_4$ and 40 inches apart. Across the break of the poop there were 4 stanchions, $5^3/_8$ x $5^3/_8$ inches, in two pairs on either side of the centreline bolted to the aft face of PA and to a 'rider' deck beam immediately over main deck beam DU. The rider and DU had the main deck planking sandwiched between them. There were two heavy stanchions, $8^3/_4$ x 9 inches, with their bottom ends halved and bolted to DV. They were also fastened to PB above and had been sawn off at deck level. They were mooring bitts.

There were six port and eleven starboard rail stanchions still standing. They tapered from $6^3/_8$ x 5 inches at the covering board to $5^1/_2$ x $4^1/_2$ inches at the under face of

Port rail with one chainplate intact and cleats, chestree and pinrail for running rigging. The latter has a moulded top edge and a protective brass strip at the bottom.

the rail. There was a $2^1/_2$ x 3 inch tenon to fit the rail. Starboard stanchion 11 had two tenons. The bottoms were mortised through the covering board and fitted on top of the frames. There was a moulding on the inside edges. The following fittings were attached to them:

Port
1. diagonal cleat
2–3. nails suggesting cleat positions
4. horizontal cleat
5. chestree
6. no fittings

Starboard
1–4. no cleats or fittings
5. 2 spikes and a mortise indicating a diagonal cleat
6–7. kevil and 2 cleats
8. 2 spikes and a mortise indicating a diagonal cleat
9. mortise for cleat and deadeye strap on outside face
10. horizontal cleat
11. chestree

There was a loose stanchion with a chestree in the fore-hold.

The massive windlass lay in the fore-hold in the bows. It must have fallen when deck beams DB and DC gave way. It was still in its original position until the early 1900s because it appeared there in a postcard of 1904. According to the *Lloyd's 1863 Survey* it would have been used with the following cables and anchors:

2	chain cables, $1^3/8$ and 1 inch diameter links, 240 and 75 fathoms long
1	hemp stream cable, $7^1/2$ inches circumference, 90 fathoms long
1	hawser, $6^1/2$ inches diameter, 90 fathoms long
3	bower anchors, 22 cwt, 21 cwt 3 stone and 20 cwt 2 stone
1	stream anchor, 7 cwt 3 stone
2	kedge, 3 cwt 2 stone and 2 cwt.

The windlass was used for anchor handling and warping the ship in and out of dock. It should be noted that according to the above survey the ship carried no capstan. This type of windlass came into general use in the 1830s and saved labour and time over the older type of handspike windlass. There were several patent versions of the pump action and the *Jhelum*'s seems to be one of the Armstrong type with the carrick bitts mortised into carlings between the two beams. These bitts, 56 high x $19^3/4$ x $5^3/4$ inches had a knee forward of which only the bolts remained and a smaller timber aft, $7^1/2$ x $6^3/4$ inches. The shaft of the windlass barrel was clamped between these two. The drums at either end were octagonal, with two iron bands. The outer bands were missing and there were two square holes for handspikes. Inside the bitts there were two drums with shaped timbers and iron rods for the cables.

The windlass lies in the fore-hold. There are holes for handspikes in the drums and the ends. The port ratchet survives and the starboard is broken off. The central gear ring engaged with the pawls.

There were eight handspike holes, two at each end on alternating faces. At the centre there were three sets of gear teeth. The outer ones had ratchets worked by levers linked to a pump mechanism that would have been mounted on top of the windlass bitt. The port ratchet had been partly snapped off. The centre gear was used with the pawls on the windlass bitt to stop the windlass running back when under load. There were five cast-iron pawls pivoted in a cast-iron frame on the aft side of the windlass bitt. The windlass bitt, 9¹/₂ x 9 inches, was once fitted at the centre of DB, resting on HB and lay on the starboard side of the forehold. It was a 'crooked' timber with a substantial curve at its lower end. It carried a large knee on its forward face and two bolts survived from this. On either side there are iron straps carrying bullseyes for the mainstay and there was a groove with a line of copper nails which showed where it passed through the main deck.

The starboard cathead for the anchor survived in crumbling condition. The port one was still in position in 1966 but had gone by 1978. The inner end of the former was fastened by a single mushroom-headed bolt through the deck planking and DA. There was a piece of lead sheet between it and the deck planking. It was also fastened to the forward side of stanchion 4 by two iron bolts and to the rail above. Outside the

Port bow, 1966, with port rails and cathead still intact. The windlass bitt was standing with planking and chock for bowsprit. Note the bullseyes for the main stay. The starboard hawsehole had a cast-iron flange which was missing by 1987. The notch in main deck beam DA may be the mortise of a carling for the companion to the crew accommodation.

rail it was supported by a hanging knee. The lower arm of the knee was attached by two iron bolts to a vertical chock fastened to the forward side of stanchion 4. There were three sheaves at its outer end.

The following ringbolts were fixed aft of the foremast carlings to the main deck beams:

DF   1 at centre
DG   1 starboard, port missing
DH   2 port and starboard
DJ   1 port, starboard missing

The ringbolts on DF and DN were used to lash down a boat or boats. In 1863, the *Jhelum* carried one long boat and two others. The latter could have been tied down with the longboat or lashed to davits on the poop. The starboard side of the poop was covered in corrugated iron and to port the evidence was inconclusive. There was a vertical rust mark forward of the first chainplate that could mark the position of the forward davit. Study of pictures of other vessels of the same date and size suggests the davits alongside the mizzen rigging were not uncommon. There was also a loose timber in the fore-hold with two ringbolts and a large ringbolt in the starboard mainmast carling, plus a number of smaller ringbolts on the sides of the ship. These will be examined in the section on rigging.

The main hatch lay between DK and DH. It measured 9 foot 7 inches athwartships and 13 feet 7$\frac{1}{2}$ inches fore and aft. The hatch had collapsed on to the rock causeway. The starboard coaming and its carling and the headledge were intact. The coamings and the carlings were fastened by four iron bolts. The coamings and headledge were halved and joined at their corners. This corner was reinforced by iron straps. The headledge top was curved and there was a notch for a portable hatch beam. The after hatch was situated between DR and DS with an opening of 4 feet 6 inches x 6 feet. The combings and headledges have disappeared. There were two short cast iron tubes, 8 inches in diameter, walls $\frac{1}{2}$ inch thick, on either side of the mainmast carlings. They passed through the deck planking and their flanges are bolted through the planking and an oblong chock by four threaded bolts. They both had tarred canvas covers secured by a length of rope. The port cover was removed to provide a canvas sample in January 1987 when the roof was repaired. The starboard one was left in situ. The purpose of these items is discussed in Chapter 11. The winch mentioned in Survey 18262 would have normally been fixed on the aft side of the main hatch. There were two timber stanchions, 6$\frac{3}{4}$ x 6$\frac{3}{4}$ inches, 47$\frac{3}{4}$ inches apart, fixed to the aft side of DO and HI which probably were its side pillars.

On the poop, there was an opening for a companionway to the accommodation below between PC and PD. This opening measured 54$\frac{1}{4}$ x 42$\frac{1}{4}$ inches. No trace of the deck structure of the companionway survived. It is likely that it had its opening athwartships with a pair of doors and a sliding hatch leading to a set of nearly vertical steps landing on the starboard side. Abaft of this, the saloon skylight survived and its outside dimensions were 63 x 69 inches. It was supported on carlings between PD and PF with 'headledges' on either side of PE. It had four turned corner posts which were

The head of the windlass bitt with the pawls and the strap and bullseye for the mainstay. A line of nails just below the pawls indicates where the bitt passed through the main deck.

rebated to receive the top, bottom and side frames. Each side was glazed and there were stumps of narrow wedge-shaped glazing bars at 8¹/₄ inch intervals on the stern side. The top edge was 3 inches deep and the bottom 2³/₄ deep, giving a glazed area 12 inches deep. There were three copper square-headed nails driven into the starboard forward frame. There were eight flat-headed copper nails driven into the starboard forward frame. There were also eight flat-headed copper nails on the fore side and a beading to hold the canvas in place that covered the top of the skylight. The top was made from six planks, 1 inch thick, and at the foreward centre was a trace of a 3-inch circular hole. At the centre aft end a 7¹/₂-inch diameter hole had been cut out, with a rebated section around which gave an overall diameter of 11 inches. This was built up with concrete over the corrugated iron. The interior of the skylight was badly charred, the forward ledge was missing and the starboard carling was in poor condition. The underside of the top had two cross-pieces and two chamfered panels with chamfered corners. When the corrugated iron, which was badly rusted, was removed from the top of the skylight a large piece of flax canvas was exposed. This had flat hand-sewn seams of the type found in sails. It was impossible to date this but it is likely that it was a part of one of the *Jhelum*'s sails. The 'glazing bars' discovered on the stern side seemed rather slight for their purpose, and there was no trace of any shuttering arrangements for protection in heavy weather. A photograph of the poop of the *Eleanor Dixon* in the 1850s in the Whitehaven Museum shows a similar skylight with small glazing bars and a protective mesh, possibly of iron rods or wire, on top of them.[2] The purpose of the two circular holes was puzzling. The larger hole was close to the steering position. It would be impossible to put a stove chimney there because it would impede the helmsman. It could be for the binnacle compass, which would have had a repeater in the saloon. Greenhill considered this position a normal one.[3] The rudder trunk established the position of the steering gear, which had disappeared. In 1849 it would have been a chain and barrel type.[4]

Notes

1.   Hackmatack, a hard pine imported from North America, a very common shipbuilding timber, rated at the same quality as pitch pine and assigned eight years by Lloyd's rules.
2.   Photograph in D. Hay, *Whitehaven, an Illustrated History* (Whitehaven, 1969).
3.   B. Greenhill, with S. Manning, *The Evolution of the Wooden Ship* (London, 1988), pp. 112–18.
4.   See model of ship *Rienzi* (1851), M.M.M.

CHAPTER TEN

MASTS AND RIGGING

None of the *Jhelum*'s masts or spars have survived. They were too useful in a port where timber and ship's fittings all had to be imported and were consequently expensive. However there were four circular piers in the *Jhelum*'s jetty that appear to have been of an earlier date than the other square piers. These could possibly have been sawn-off sections of her masts. Ship's spars and timbers were frequently recycled in the harbour. The disused jetty out to the *Actaeon* and the *Charles Cooper* re-used the spars of the French barque *Fennia* for longitudinals. Even with the absence of the masts and spars it was still possible to identify the positions of three masts from their chainplates, carlings or mast partners attached to the deck beams or, in their absence, the mortises cut in the deck beams. A substantial amount of the standing rigging was found in the forehold and some of the belaying points for the running rigging could be identified from the foremast pinrails, fairleads, cleats and ringbolts. Ringbolts and the strops for the bullseyes assisted on the layout of the bowsprit's standing rigging. Contemporary sources on masting and rigging, especially Fincham and Kipping's works, and paintings and models, together with the *Lloyd's Survey* of 1863 fill out the picture. The National Maritime Museum also holds a rigging plan of the Liverpool built ship *Meg of Meldon* of 1840.

There is no reason to suppose that the *Jhelum* was anything but conventional in rig. She was launched as a ship and cut down to a barque in 1858. It was fashionable to split the deep traditional single topsails into two sails after about 1865–6. It was unlikely the *Jhelum* was converted, because of her relatively small size, although there were 19th-century sailing ships of smaller tonnage carrying double topsails. The *Lloyd's Survey* of 1863 simply noted the existence of topsails. The photograph of the two wooden barques of about the *Jhelum*'s size at anchor at the Chincha Islands taken in 1861 showed that they both had single topsails. There was no rush to convert every square rigger to the new layout although it was much handier and less labour-intensive than the old one. The 1863 *Lloyd's Survey* also stated that the *Jhelum*'s standing rigging was hemp and not wire; and yet all the shrouds and backstays in the fore-hold were in wire rope. There is no doubt that they were from the *Jhelum* and not dumped from some other vessel, as sometimes happened in the Falklands. The chainplates and deadeyes attached to them matched the ones still in situ. The rerigging in wire must have been carried out after 1863. It was also possible that only the foremast was rerigged with wire rope, perhaps after the damage to the rigging in the River Plate in 1869. But one deadeye attached to a length of wire rope was found in the hold under the poop

This port view of the poop shows the five surviving mizzen chainplates and the two original ports. The first lies forward of the third chainplate and the second just aft of the large opening cut out after the *Jhelum* had been hulked. Nine strakes of the topside planking have been lost. This was probably caused by rot because they lie in a sheltered position clear of the intertidal zone.

accommodation. This suggests but does not confirm that the mizzen, and therefore all three masts, were rigged with wire.

The bowsprit was fitted between the knightheads and its heel was positioned against a wedge-shaped chock fixed against the forward side of the windlass (bitt). This fitting was observed in 1978 but had disappeared with the collapsed pawl bitt into the hold. The steeve of the bowsprit was conventionally between 20° and 30° and the angle of the top of the *Jhelum*'s stempost fore and aft was about 18°.[1] The remains of the chainplate for the bobstay were still attached to the stem and the two bullseye strops fixed to the outer faces of the knightheads served to attach the bowsprit shrouds to the bow. There were two more on starboard rail stanchions 8 and 9. These were anchorage points for the jib-boom guys, which would have been led there via a whisker boom fastened to the cathead.[2]

The foremast was stepped between main deck beams DD and DF with DE as a half beam. The position was indicated by the mortises for its carlings. It was set further back from the stem than in similar vessels of the first three decades of the 19th century. The whaler *Baffin*, built at Liverpool in 1819, makes a good comparison, with her foremast about one-eighth of her length from stem to sternpost compared with the *Jhelum*'s one-sixth. This was yet another feature that showed that the *Jhelum* was no 18th-century look-alike and that the design of her type had progressed, albeit slowly.

The main mast was stepped between main deck beams DN and DO and the mizzen between DU and DV. In 1849, all three would have consisted of main, top and topgallant masts. When the *Jhelum* was cut down to a barque in 1858, she would have been stripped of her mizzen yards and probably the top and topgallant masts.

Both Fincham and Kipping have tables of dimensions for vessels of about the *Jhelum*'s size (Tables 10.1 and 10.2).[3] Fincham based his mast dimensions on the breadth of the vessel and his ones for yards on the length, while Kipping based his on the tonnage. Fincham has been used to give an idea of the *Jhelum*'s spars as a ship. His nearest equivalent was a ship of 123 feet length and 27 feet breadth. Kipping's were for a barque of 420 tons. Neither specified these measurements precisely and there was quite a difference between the two sets of figures. The *Jhelum* probably retained all her fore and main-mast spars, and possibly her mizzen mast when she was reduced to a barque. Tables 10.1 and 10.2 must therefore be treated with caution.

Table 10.1 Fincham's dimensions for a ship 123 long, 27 breadth
(all dimensions in feet)

Main mast 52.9 hounded, 10.6 head, 17.05 housed, total 80.55
Main yard 63.8, 2.66 arm, total 69.12
Main top-mast 32.75 hounded, 5.3 headed, total 38.05
Main top-sail yard 44.1, 3.67 arm, total 51.44
Main top-gallant mast 16.65 hounded, 2.4 headed, total 19.05
Main top-gallant yard 27.8, 1.19 arm, total 28.99
Main royal mast 10.6 pole (in one piece with top-gallant)
Main royal yard 19.7, 0.76 arm, total 20.46

Foremast 47.55 hounded, 9.6 headed, 16 housed, total 73.15
Fore yard 57.45, 2.4 arm, total 62.25
Fore top-mast 29.4 hounded, 4.8 headed, total 34.2
Fore top-sail yard 39.7, 3.32 arm, total 43.02
Fore top-gallant mast 14.95 hounded, 2.8 headed, total 17.75
Fore top-gallant yard 25.08, 1.05 arm, total 27.18
Fore royal mast 9.5 pole
Fore royal yard 17.9, 0.66 arm, total 18.41

Mizzen mast 44.2 hounded, 7.15 headed, 15.6 housed, total 66.95
Cross-jack yard 39.7, 1.71 arm, total 43.12
Mizzen top-mast 20.65 hounded, 2.95 headed, total 23.6
Mizzen top-sail yard 27.43, 2.31 arm, total 32.05
Mizzen top-gallant mast 10.25 hounded, 1.6 housed, total 11.85
Mizzen top-gallant yard 17.63, 0.71 arm, total 18.34
Mizzen royal 6.52 pole
Mizzen royal yard 12.7, 0.52 arm, total 13.74

Bowsprit 35.88
Jib-boom 25.55
Flying jib-boom 27.65
Driver (or spanker) boom 44.4
Driver (or spanker) gaff 33.5
Try-sail gaff 11.05
Main try-sail-gaff 22
Swing boom 38.3 (for studding sails)
Spritsail yard 39.7, 1.71 arm, total 43.12

Table 10.2 Kipping's dimensions for a 420-ton barque

Barque of 420 tons

Dimensions of Ship:
Length, 113 ft.; Breadth 28 ft

Names of the Masts and yards	Masts or booms			Yards		
	Extreme Length	Headed Length	Diameter	Extreme Length	Arm	Diameter
	Ft. In.	Ft. In.	Ins.	Ft. In.	Ft. In.	Ins.
Main mast and yard	63 0	9 8	$20^1/_2$	52 0	3 8	13
Top-mast and yard	35 0	5 0	$13^1/_4$	43 0	3 0	$10^1/_2$
Topgallant mast and yard	17 6		8	33 0	2 4	$7^1/_2$
Royal-mast and yard	10 6		4	23 0	1 9	$5^3/_4$
Fore-mast and yard	60 6	9 8	20	52 0	3 8	13
Top-mast and yard	35 0	5 0	$13^1/_4$	43 0	3 0	$10^1/_2$
Topgallant-mast and yard	17 6		8	33 0	2 4	$7^1/_2$
Royal-mast and yard	10 6		4	23 0	1 9	$5^3/_4$
Mizzen mast	62 0	8 0	$16^1/_2$			
Top-mast	35 0		$9^3/_4$			
Pole	9	8				
Bowsprit	34 9		21			
Jib-boom	38 0		12			
Flying-jibboom	39 0		8			
Mizzen-boom		35 0		9		
Gaff	30 0		$7^1/_2$			
Main and Fore-gaffs	21 0		$8^3/_4$			

The existence of topmasts and topgallants was confirmed by the number of

The remains of the wire shrouds and backstays of the foremast buried in the fore-hold with parts of four chainplates and a deadeye.

chainplates per mast. There were five large ones for the shrouds and three smaller for the backstays on the fore and main. There would have been two for the topmasts, one for the topgallant masts. The royal backstay was often set up inside the bulwarks. The mizzen had six chainplates: four for shrouds and two for backstays.

Most of the chainplates and their strops and deadeyes have disappeared. Their positions were indicated by the stumps of the chainplate and preventer bolts. On the foremast, the chainplates for number 1 port and number 4 starboard shrouds were complete with strops for their deadeyes, which were missing. Numbers 2, 5, 7 and 8 to port, and 1, 2, 5 and 6 to starboard were incomplete. The backstay chainplates were a single rod and the shrouds double. None of the mainmast chainplates were in situ, probably because they would have interfered with the laying of the roof. The same was true on the mizzen starboard side, while to port numbers 1, 2, 3 and 5 were complete single rods but without strops, number 4 was incomplete and the position of number 6 was marked by its bolts. The latter bolts were worn down, which suggested that this last pair of backstays was taken off when she was changed to barque rig. Three complete chainplates with their deadeyes were found in the forehold between HF and HG. One of these was embedded in a mass of wire rigging together with two more chainplates. A fourth was broken but with a strop attached. The latter was taken as a sample for further examination and preservation at Merseyside Maritime Museum. It was a fine specimen of blacksmithing, with two grooves forged into its outer surface and a mushroom-headed bolt locked by a wedge to fasten it to the chainplate. Another chainplate had been recorded lying in the water off the starboard side. The chainplates passed through a mortise cut in the rail, which was unusual. Most rigging diagrams showed them in a slot of the outside edge of the rail. It has been stated that the *Jhelum* had channels, which were stout wooden platforms to angle the chainplates out from the hull. There was absolutely no evidence for these and the straight chainplates demonstrated this fact. An old watercolour of the *Jhelum* showed, however, that the chainplates had protective rubbing pieces of timber that could be mistaken for channels.[4] Shroud deadeyes measured $8^5/4$ inches in diameter and backstay ones $6^3/8$ inches. The diameter of the wire rope of the shrouds was $1^1/4$ inches and of the back stays 1 inch. The evidence for the bowsprit's standing rigging has already been mentioned. The two bullseyes attached to either side of the windlass bitt were evidence of the fixing position of the mainstay and that it was double where it had to pass round the foremast.

None of the running rigging has survived. It was probably salvaged when the ship was hulked. The remaining fragments of the port and starboard forward rails had evidence of belaying points and ring bolts for blocks. There was also a chestree for the foresail sheet on port rail stanchion 4 and another similar one which was presumably from the starboard side was lying in the fore-hold. The latter also contained a probable foremast carling with two ringbolts, and there was a ringbolt fastened through the starboard main-mast carling. On the outside of the hull to port there was a small ringbolt near main deck beam DK, and another just aft of the last mizzen chainplate bolt. On the port stern quarter, two large bolts indicated the existence of a wooden chock for a ringbolt for the lower block of the mainsail braces. The purpose of the two aforementioned small ringbolts was not so clear. It is possible that they were used to fasten blocks to handle the sheets of studding sails; and it is likely that the *Jhelum* was fitted with these light-weather sails. These various fittings, combined with the evidence of the standing rigging and contemporary practice, suggest that the *Jhelum* had the following sails:

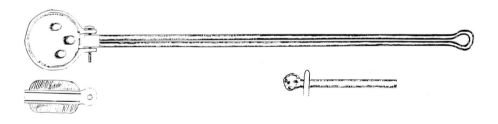

Fore-mast shroud chainplate.

Bowsprit: fore top-mast staysail, jib, and flying jib and spritsail referred
                        to in the *Official Log* in August 1864 when the drunken mate
was 'laying on the rails, bowsprit or spritsail yard.'

Foremast: fore course, topsail, topgallant and royal with studding sails on
                        fore topsail and topgallant sails

Main staysails: topmast, topgallant royal and storm lower staysails

Mainmast: mainsail, topsail, topgallant and royal with studding sails on
                        main, topsail and topgallant sails and main topsail

Mizzen staysails: topsail and topgallant staysails

Mizzen-mast: (as ship) topsail, topgallant and royal sails and spanker
                        (as barque) spanker and topsail

The belaying points on the rails for the bowsprit and foremast sails going from the
bow towards the stern could have been as follows:

1.   Diagonal mortises for cleats on starboard rail stanchions numbers 5 and 8 for
     stay sail or jib sheets
2.   Kevil on starboard rail stanchions numbers 6 and 7 for mooring warps
3.   Chestree and cleat on port stanchion 4 for fore-sheet
4.   Carling ring bolts in fore-hold for topsail sheets
5.   Port pin rail 12 of the 17 holes could be accounted for thus:
     1.   foresail leech lines and bunt lines
     2.   foresail clew garnets
     3.   fore topsail bunt lines and clew lines
     4.   fore topgallant sheets
     5.   fore topgallant bunt and clew lines
     6.   fore topsail halliard
     7.   fore royal sheets
     8.   fore royal bunt lines and clew lines
     9.   inner jib halliard
     10. flying jib halliard
     11. fore royal halliard
     12. fore lazy sheet

Notes

1.   R. de Kerchove, *An International Maritime Dictionary* (New York, 1948).
2   H. Underhill, *Rigging the Clipper Ship and Ocean Carrier* (Glasgow, 1946) p. 11, fig.8.
3.   R. Kipping, *Masting and Rigging* (London, 1866, 10th edn); J. Fincham, *A Treatise on Masting Ships
     and Mast Making; Explaining their Principles and Practical Operations, the Mode of Forming and Combining
     Made-masts etc., etc.,* (London, 1843), pp. 145,147.
4.   M. Bound, 'The Hulk Jhelum, a Derivative Expression of Late British Indiaman Building,' *International
     Journal of Nautical Archaeology and Underwater Exploration*, Vol XIX (1), p. 44 and Vol XX (2), p. 171.

CHAPTER ELEVEN

CREW ACCOMMODATION AND CARGO SPACE

CREW ACCOMMODATION

The crew lived forward in every sailing ship of the *Jhelum*'s period. The only alternative would have been a deckhouse. The *Jhelum* did not have such accommodation. The stripping of the hull when hulked and over a century's deterioration meant that little evidence of the crew's quarters and its fittings survived. It extended from the apron to the aft side of hold beam HC. Two surviving iron spikes on the port side suggested that there was a bulkhead of vertical boards at that point to separate it from the cargo hold. It was floored by $2^1/_2$-inch-thick pine planking. One small section had not been removed. This lay between hold beams HB and HC up against the starboard-side waterway. The access would have been via a scuttle or hatch on the main deck. As main deck beams DA, DB and DC had all collapsed, its position could not be ascertained. However Karl Kortum's photograph of the *Jhelum*'s bows in 1966 show these beams intact and the port side of HB had a mortise cut in it for a carling. On the other hand, contemporary practice suggests that the access would have been on the centre line.[1] The total floor area was about 175 square feet, which would have been cramped even for the reduced crew. It was possible that the carpenter, boatswain and the cook-steward lived aft, either in the poop or in a boarded-off space in the tween-decks of the hold – 'the steerage'. The crew probably slept in hammocks, for there was no evidence of bunk uprights or rails. On the other hand, the semi-circular 'fairlead' nailed to the forward side of main deck beam DD looked as if it could have been used to rig a tarpaulin over a hammock to defend the sleeper from the leaking deck. The only other features of note were the two scupper holes between hold beams HB and HC. The nearest HB retained its lead lining and the other had a circle of copper nails where the lining had been ripped out. These were both similar to scupper pipes in the poop accommodation. The bowl of a pewter spoon was found between the third and fourth port-side cant frames. Other features noted, but which could not be explained, were a shallow horizontal groove, 3 x $^1/_2$ inch deep from the

apron to main deck beam DA in the port and starboard ceilings. There was no trace of
the galley and this was probably washed away in the storm of August 1870.

The aft accommodation occupied the poop and had its own deck. The main structural features have already been described. Much of the layout was clear, but many
smaller features had been destroyed or damaged by the fire of 1983, which seems to
have started between poop deck beams PC and PD. At this point, the ceiling, frames
and external planking were burnt through. Access was via a companionway between
PC and PD: the carlings for this were still in position. The main space – 'the saloon' –
was illuminated by the skylight. There were nine deck lights, three side ports (two to
port and one to starboard, with possibly another one in the burnt area) and four stern
windows. The space around the central 'saloon' was partitioned into cabins and stores.
The position of the partitions was marked in the underside of the poop deck and the
panelling over the arms of the lodging staple knees and mouldings between the deck

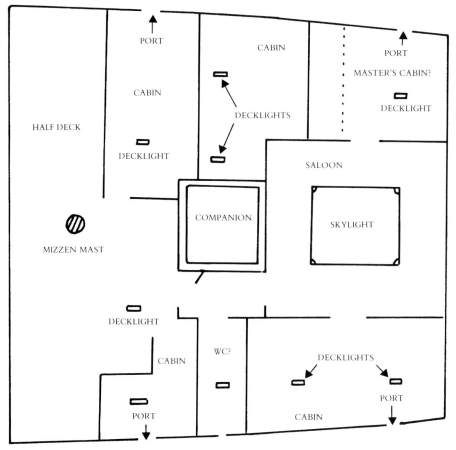

Stern accommodation plan.

The charred interior of the poop skylight has faint traces of two panels with rounded-off corners. The large hole was probably for a tell-tale compass below the binnacle and the smaller one may have been for the chimney of a coal stove. Poop deck beam PE has been cut away where it crossed the skylight opening. Note the decorative turned corner posts.

beams. On the port side between PD and PE there was a broken brass ring fixed into the underside of the deck planking. This looked as if it was used for hanging an oil lamp.

On the port side there were two lead-lined scupper holes and a third to starboard similar to those on the starboard side of the crew's accommodation. A hatch immediately forward of the sternpost and transom beam gave access to the hold. It was noted that its framing was rounded, perhaps to ease the passing of ship's stores in casks.

The after accommodation followed the general pattern of stern accommodation for merchant ships of the early 19th century. It was compared with other contemporary accommodation plans which included:

1.   Plan of Liverpool-built whaler *Baffin* (1820) at Whitby Museum.
2.   Plan of Schooners *Bonanza, Tampico* and *Mazeppa*, built at Whitehaven 1830-3, in Brocklebank Collection, Merseyside Maritime Museum.
3.   Plan of Bristol-built ship *Victoria* (1831), Science Museum, negative number 6116.
4.   The whaler *Charles W. Morgan* (1841), preserved at Mystic Seaport, Maine, USA.

All these examples show a central space next to the stern, with cabins to port and starboard. Forward of this was a separate central space with a companionway to the deck above. The *Jhelum*'s accommodation was laid out in this way. She also had a raised 'half-deck' area at the break of the poop and this was probably for storage, or a sail locker. Against this idea, the *Official Log* for 17th March 1870 referred to sails being moved out of the hold. It was also possible that it could have been used as sleeping accommodation for the boatswain, cook-steward and carpenter. Stevens defined such an area as 'the half-deck' and that was the traditional accommodation for apprentices.[2] There were five cabins, possibly a pantry and a WC. The aft one on the port side is the largest and was lit by a port light, part of a stern window and two deck lights. Between this and the forward port cabin was a long narrow space 30 inches wide which was a WC. The hole for the outlet pipe had been cut through the port ceiling between the frames and through the outer planking. The forward port cabin had a side light and the lodging knee and poop stanchion at PB had been cut away for a bunk or fixed piece of furniture.

The partitions dividing the spaces were fixed between the mortises in the deck and the timber upstands on the deck head. The shape of the mortises suggests there were solid pillars framing horizontal or vertical tongue-and-groove boards. In 1978, a small piece of $^{13}/_{16}$-inches thick tongued-and-groove board was found attached to the aft side of poop deck beam PC. It was destroyed in the fire. Vertical boards were found on the wreck of a mid-19th-century brig.[3] The *Charles W. Morgan*'s partitions had mouldings as well.

Starboard side of the poop accommodation between deck beams PD (left) and PE (right). The 'shadow' of a locker or possibly an athwartships bunk is visible on the ceiling. Note the four small uprights below the clamp. Their purpose is unknown. At the top of the picture two sections of timber are visible, one to the left of centre and a smaller piece next to PE. These were used to fix the upper ends of a partition.

Starboard side of the poop accommodation between deck beams PE and PF. This was the area of the aftermost starboard cabin with its square port at the centre of the picture. Above there is an air space with uprights framing the side of the counter and the iron staple knee. Note the junction between the top of the fashion timber, the wing and rider transoms, the large knee and the horn timbers in the bottom right corner.

It was probable that the 'saloon' was the master's day cabin, and his rights to this space were noted in Chapter 4. The space forward of this with the companionway was probably a general dining area, with fixed table and benches. To give enough space for these furnishings the companionway was probably a near-vertical ladder. Some ships had a semi-circular set of stairs. The port after-cabin was probably the master's because it was the largest and best lit.

On the other hand, the master was traditionally accommodated on the starboard side. The forward port cabin could have been the steward's because it was common practice to berth the steward on the same side as the master. This would leave two of the starboard ones for the first mate and second mate (or boatswain) with one spare. There were also apprentices, and on the last voyage a single passenger. Perhaps some of the cabins had double bunks. The cabins were tiny by modern standards but nevertheless were acceptable at the time, providing little more than a bunk and space for a sea chest. The decoration of the under-deck and the skylight with moulded panels was white and conformed with contemporary practice. In 1978, a small area of blue wall-paper was found on the ceiling of the aft starboard cabin. It could be a later addition after 1871, but there seemed no good reason why anyone would want to decorate a store or workshop in this way. There were virtually no remains of any furnishings. On the starboard side, also in the aft cabin, there was a mark on the ceiling which might have been evidence for a cross locker fixed to the forward partition. It was probable that the bunks were fitted fore and aft, against the ceiling. The end of the main deck waterway on the port side had an extension timber on the end. They both could have supported a bunk. The change of colour in the ceiling at PB suggests that there was a bulkhead between the cabins and the 'half deck'. Finally, the *Official Log Book* for 30th December 1863 has an interesting reference. The captain came on board and found that the lock of his cabin door had been picked. The medicine chest and a locker containing wines and spirits had been broken into. The miscreant turned out to be the boatswain because a bottle of vinegar and a bottle of laudanum were found in his 'berth'. This gave some indication of the contents of the captain's cabin and definitely implied that the boatswain lived in the poop.

THE CARGO SPACE

The *Jhelum* must have been built with a tween-deck because of the amount of general cargo she carried up to 1863. The *Lloyd's Register Survey* does not mention one in 1863. This suggests that part or all the tween-decks were taken out in or about 1863 when she carried mainly bulk cargoes outwards and homewards. The way in which the present 'tween-deck' under the corrugated iron roof was fitted and nailed was not up to the standard of ship carpentry in the rest of the vessel. The planks themselves, though stout 3-inch-thick pieces of pine have a new 'look' to them as well, with no signs of wear and tear. There was evidence of light bulkheads in the hold at the bow and the stern. These could have been to provide space for the ship's stores or to prevent the guano from moving into the ends of the vessel. At the starboard end of hold beam HB, two vertical boards were found still in position nailed up against a triangular timber shaped to fit against the ceiling. After in the poop hold there were two small timbers nailed to the port ceiling between PHB and PHC that could have been part of the aft bulkhead. Both were too flimsy to be considered as bulkheads in the sense of an anti-collision bulkhead. They were not that nor was it usual to provide such a feature on a wooden sailing ship. They were generally temporary arrangements according to R.W. Stevens.[4] Hold beams HK and HL, which were not directly below the after hatch, have been rounded off and worn by successive cargoes being dropped and shifted on them. This showed that the *Jhelum*'s tween deck planking had been removed at some point while she was sailing with cargoes.

The cargo space also contained space for stowing the anchor cables, the pumps and two iron water tanks. The cable locker was usually sited aft of the windlass, with two spurling pipes to lead the cable off the deck. It was considered that the two short cast-iron tubes on either side of the main mast were for the cables. The *Admiral Moorson* had the chain locker in this position. However, they are 8 inches in diameter, which is much wider than necessary for $1^{3}/_{8}$-inch diameter chain cable. There was also the problem of the position of the pumps. In most sailing ships, the pumps were fitted immediately abaft the main mast, but the *Jhelum* has two large wrought-iron water tanks where the pumps would have been sited. It therefore looks as if the cast-iron tubes housed the pump barrels. These were cast iron and being of a slightly smaller diameter would have been wedged in position. They could be removed easily and were when the ship was hulked. There has been some debate about whether or not

The remains of the fore bulkhead on the starboard side of the hold.

these tanks were original or were fitted after the *Jhelum*'s arrival at Stanley. It has been suggested that they were perhaps used to store petrol or whale, penguin or seal oil. The small boiler found in the hold near HJ looked as if some kind of boiling process had taken place on board. To counter this, the tanks were of a type of construction that used very large hand-fitted rivets, suggesting a mid-19th century rather than late 19th-century date of building. Their forward ends were fitted under hold beam HJ. If they had been fitted afterwards the deck beam would have simply been sawn away to make space for the full height of the tank. Besides all this, there was no documentary evidence for any boiling of oil in Stanley. Oil was certainly shipped in from Camp in barrels.[5] On the other hand, the siting of iron water tanks amidships was well documented for iron ships and Stevens noted: 'Fixed tanks containing enough for the crew, are now generally placed on the keelson, near the pump well or chain locker.' He also warned about the risk that the weight of heavy tanks placed in the centre of the ship could open the garboard strakes, especially if the tanks had leaked and let fresh water on to them, for fresh water would make them rot.[6]

The *Jhelum* must have been fitted with the tanks from new because of the kind of cargoes she was expected to carry. Water casks were notorious for leaking, especially in the tropics, and such leakage could cause serious damage to cargoes of cotton, nitrates and guano. The high cost of buying fresh supplies of water in ports such as Arica and Callao may have been another consideration. The two tanks' combined capacity was about 4,000 gallons. The daily water ration under the Official Agreement

The starboard water tank from the starboard side. The carlings hold the tank in place and the forward end has been made to fit under hold beam HJ. The top and sides were badly corroded.

was 3 quarts a man. With a maximum of twenty on board this would have amounted to a daily consumption of 15 gallons and this in turn meant that theoretically they held sufficient water for 266 days, enough for a round voyage to the west coast of South America. In practice, the daily consumption was probably higher and there was wastage and evaporation to be accounted for as well. The 19 tons of water and the weight of the tanks themselves would make a useful contribution to the ballast needed when carrying a general cargo outward with a high proportion of light goods such as textiles. It looked as if there was a balancing pipe between the two tanks because both had pipes at their bottoms at their forward ends. In the absence of such a device consuming one tank before the other could have affected stability. Internally they had three braces and a thin cement coating. The latter was to stop the water becoming contaminated with rust and becoming 'ship's port wine'. According to Stevens, such water was not dangerous but did need to be filtered before drinking. There was an oval inspection opening, 15 inches across, and two lead pipes passing through riveted, badly corroded iron flanges in the forward centre corner. The two inlet or outlet pipes were $2^1/_2$ inches and about $^3/_4$ inches in diameter. The tanks were made from $^5/_8$ inch wrought-iron plate. The starboard tank, which was examined in detail, had large sections missing on top and on its starboard side. Both tanks were presumably bedded on a platform fastened to the top of the keelson. They both had carlings of crooked timber, probably English oak, to hold them in position to port and starboard.

Notes

1. See plan of *Admiral Moorsom* (1827) in D.R. MacGregor, *Merchant Sailing Ships 1815–50* (London, 1984), fig. 115 or models of the ship *Rienzi* (1851), M.M.M.
2. R.W. Stevens, *On the Stowage of Ships and their Cargoes* (London and Plymouth, 7the edn, 1893), p. 331.
3. Surveyed by the M.M.M. at Ainsdale, Southport, after being exposed by very high tides in 1988.
4. Ibid, p. 329; MacGregor, *Merchant Sailing Ships*, p. 147, quotes naval architect J. Bennett's comment in the mid-1820s that iron tanks were replacing wooden casks.
5. Falkland Islands Company Archives, Accounts 1st July 1872: 'sold to Packe (owner of the hulk *Jhelum*) 2 barrels of penguin oil, 1 of penguin fat, 1 railway truck and rails for Fox Bay, £14 8s 0d.'
6. Stevens, *On the Stowage of Ships*, p. 785.

CHAPTER TWELVE

THE *JHELUM* AS A
HULK

When Captain Beaglehole sailed away from Stanley in HMS *Charybdis* in May 1871, he left the *Jhelum* at anchor in Stanley harbour. A photograph taken in March 1871 to record the visit of the Duke of Edinburgh's ship, HMS *Galatea*, showed her moored east of the Falkland Island Company's jetty. The Company's records suggest that she was not moved to her present position until about 1873–4 when she was bought by the Packe brothers to serve their Stanley residence, Sulivan House. The Packes were important figures in the life of the colony. They controlled large tracts of land at Fitzroy, Port Louis and on West Falkland and were responsible for introducing sheep farming to the islands. They supplied beef to visiting ships in competition with the FIC. In March 1871, it was Edward Packe who led the Duke of Edinburgh on a shooting expedition 50 miles south of Stanley and in June he offered to sell his 16-ton cutter, the *Exe*, which had been built at Exmouth in 1868 for £300, to the Government for a pilot boat.[1]

   Sulivan House was a substantial residence which the Packes used when attending to their own business and Legislative Council business in Stanley, and the *Jhelum* was a useful adjunct to the property because she provided a wharf and a warehouse for their inter-island cargoes. That the hulk was clearly linked to the house was shown by their combined sale in 1922. The reason for the sale was because Vere Packe, a descendant of the two brothers, had lost his son and heir in a flying accident in 1919 while serving in the Royal Flying Corps. As a result, the Packe properties at Fitzroy, Port Louis and Stanley were all offered for sale. The FIC bought the Stanley property (including a hulk and a jetty) to stop it falling to a Senor Menendez of Punta Arenas, Chile, a potential business competitor. In 1923, the FIC sold it to the Colonial Government.[2]

   The first map to show the *Jhelum* in her present position is an Admiralty survey of 1891 in the collection of the Falkland's museum. There is no evidence of how she was moved up the harbour. Perhaps she was moved using an anchor and windlass or was towed by rowing boats. There was certainly no steam tug available in the harbour at that time. It would be interesting to know if she was stripped of her gear before or after she was beached. It is likely that much of the re-usable, easily removable equipment such as sails, boats, steering gear, winch, upper masts and spars was removed close to the FIC's stores and workshops for they probably had the most use for such materials. The standing rigging was abandoned in the hold, and the forward deck planking was probably re-used, perhaps in the house or in building the jetty. Timber was a much-valued commodity in Stanley for it all had to be imported, and there have been examples of re-used ship's timbers around the town in houses, sheds and fencing. Once the *Jhelum* was beached the two large loading port openings were cut through the midships part of the hull to provide access to a small vessel tied up alongside the starboard side from the jetty. A large quantity of locally quarried stone was tipped into the hold to provide an anchor to stop her floating off and to form a causeway between the two loading ports. This was finished off with a wooden deck. The after and poop decks were retained as a roof and a large quantity of tar was brushed on them to stop leaks. The two cast-iron tubes for the pumps were covered with sailcloth canvas. The skylight over the saloon was retained for light, but all the internal partitions and doors of the poop cabins were stripped out. Eventually, a stove chimney was built through the hole left by the removal of the binnacle and the tell-tale compass. Windows were cut on either side. To port they were between deck beams DE and DQ, DT and DU, PE and PF. To starboard, they were between DT and DU, PE and PF.

Access from the hold to the poop was created by cutting through the centres two of the deck beams, DV and PHA, at the break of the poop. This was fitted with a door. There was a door and screen across the after section at hold beam HI. The starboard loading port also had doors and there was a fence with a gate on the jetty itself. Some of these features may be later, perhaps after the Government's takeover.

The original deck planking eventually became too rotten and was covered with corrugated iron. The starboard side was also sheeted over at the same time. The rails and stanchions of this after section were sawn off to make room for this roof. It was in position by 1888. The forward section was left to rot. All the rails minus the bulwark planking were still standing and the windlass was still on deck in a photograph taken about 1920.[3] The opening in the starboard bow between deck beams DA and DB was to accommodate a lavatory for the joiners who worked in the aft section. It was connected by a walkway along the starboard side of the deck beams. The nails for fastening its planks were found fixed in the tops of the deck beams.[4] The joiner's shop could have been introduced when the government took over the house and the hulk in 1923. Older residents, including Mrs S. Miller of Lois Cottage, Stanley, remember it in use as a workshop in the 1920s and 1930s. In 1978, there were still many wood shavings in the poop, together with a narrow bench under the stern windows. The treadle lathe found in the hold near hold beam HN may have been from the joiner's shop. On the port side of the after-hold a painted inscription read: 'W. Morley C. Evans repairs 17th April 1930. Morley Evans Finish Repairs Never.' This had disappeared after the fire in 1983. It was not clear what repairs were referred to. It could have been the renewal of the corrugated iron.

The joiner's shop was possibly abandoned when the *Jhelum* became the Government's petrol store. She was serving as such in 1948.[5] Petrol and later aviation fuel was stored in drums. The door between the poop and the after hold has crudely painted on it in red lead, 'Danger No Smoking.' The gates on the jetty also had a post with a sign attached but the wording had been obliterated. In 1951, the loading port was tried as an embarkation point for the island's first seaplane, Norseman 5VP-FAD.[6] It continued as a government store until about 1964. The poop contained redundant gas lamps and the hold building materials. Some of the corrugated asbestos roofing

The 'boiler' (left) and its 'firebox' (right) lie on the port side of the hold between hold beams HI and HJ. The latter is lying on top of the flywheel of a treadle lathe.

sheets recorded in the tween-deck in Karl Kortum's 1966 photographs were found lying in the port side of the hold between hold beams HL and HN. Kortum's pictures in fact show that the covered area had been emptied out of everything except for these roofing sheets and two packing cases. Chemicals, including formaldehyde left over from an expedition, were also stored and the steel cylinder found in the hold near the starboard side of hold beam HM could have had a chemical use. It was similar to the back-pack containers used for spraying insecticides in the 1930s.[7]

There were a large number of other finds in the hold. In among the mud, sand and rock there was a considerable quantity of glass bottles, fragments of pottery, tiles, brick, window glass, and domestic metal objects such as a broken candlestick and a knife grinder. The bottles included large numbers of green glass 'elephant' beer bottles, and whisky and wine bottles. There were also seven complete and two fragments of the 'codd' type of soda water bottle. The latter was marked 'sibern. . .'. Other marked bottles included: 'J. Walker Kilmarnock', 'Lea and Perrins, Worcester Works', 'Elliman's Embrocation' and 'Atkinson, London'. They all appear to date from the late 19th century. Most of the pottery fragments were not stamped or marked. There were pieces of the distinctive white earthenware jars of Keiller's marmalade. Again these could not be precisely dated.

Four pieces, however, proved to be of more interest. The first was a piece of a large earthenware flowerpot stamped 'Royal Pottery, Weston Super Mare.' There were a large number of pieces of this type of pot among the rocks of the loading port causeway. The pottery had been founded in 1836 and by the mid-19th century was acknowledged as the makers of the best pots available, producing pots for export worldwide as well as for Kew Gardens and the royal palaces. After the death of Matthews, their second manager in 1888, the factory appears to have gone into a decline. The second was a fragment of vitreous lead-glazed earthenware with a classical grotesque border with the printed mark for John Meir & Son's Greengates pottery, Tunstall. This factory was in operation between 1837 and 1897. The particular border pattern has been identified as 'leader' and dates from between 1870 and 1880. The third was a fragment of lead-glazed white earthenware, underglazed blue, printed with part of a seascape executed in stipple-and-line engraving. It could be part of the 'Views of Bristol' series made by Pountney and Allies, or their successors at Temple Backs, Bristol, and was perhaps produced about 1835–40. Finally, there was a fragment of lead-glazed white earthenware, under-glazed blue, printed with a flowers-and-leaves pattern with a shallow footrim. It was possibly made by Henshall Williamson & Co of Longport or the Herculaneum Pottery of Liverpool and it might have dated to 1820–5 but could be later.[8]

The *Jhelum* in 1964 when still in use as a store. Note that the gates and the partition across the loading port were still in use. The jetty was in good condition and the round piers (possibly ship's spars) are visible close to the hulk. The rails were almost all intact.

An oval brass label stamped 'McIvor, Birkenhead' was another interesting find. Its Merseyside connection at first suggested that it came with the ship in 1871. But according to the trade directories the firm was not established until about 1875. It remained in business until about 1964. In 1875 the firm was a ship cementer, and dealer in firebricks and holy stones. It built furnace arches, laid galley floors, cleaned boilers, bilges and flues, and scraped and painted ships' hulls. Later it took up precision and structural engineering, and became a steel and builder's merchant. The label must have been part of the material dumped in the hold after 1875. Finally, a cast-iron, open-topped boiler or cauldron was found next to the treadle lathe. Its walls were 2 inches thick and there was a tapping hole at the bottom. It had originally been mounted on its own furnace which lay next to it. Its purpose was unknown. The miscellaneous nature and the origin of all this mass of material was a puzzle. As a body it was later than the ship and its abandonment. The pottery was of a higher quality and less robust than one would have expected on board. Equally, there was no record of the *Jhelum* carrying bottles, etc, as cargo on the last voyage. It was therefore concluded that this material was introduced from elsewhere after 1873–4. The obvious source was Sulivan House. As Stanley had no rubbish collection until relatively recently most residents dug pits in their back gardens to dispose of inorganic materials that could not be burnt. The Packes did not have to resort to digging in the garden, their rubbish could be simply tipped into the hold of the *Jhelum*.[9]

Notes

1. Captain R.C. Packe came to the Islands about 1850; his brother Edward joined him in 1866. The latter pioneered sheep farming and the former was the Island's senior JP. Sulivan House was bought from Captain B.J. Sulivan. See V.F. Boyson, *The Falkland Islands* (Oxford, 1924), pp. 152–3, 184.
2. Falkland Islands Company records, Despatches No. 4, 14th January 1871 and No. 8, 14th March 1871. S. Miller, 'The History of the Falkland Islands Company', *Falkland Islands Journal*, 1986, pp. 39–49 and Falkland Islands Government Land Registry records.
3. Photograph by V.F. Boyson.
4. Information from Tony Carey, who used to be in charge of stores on the *Jhelum*.
5. G.L. Garratt, 'Hulks at Port Stanley, Falkland Islands', *Sea Breezes*, new series, Vol. V, p. 310.
6. Information from John Smith, Curator of the Falkland Islands Museum and D.A. Rough, 'The History of the Falkland Islands Government Air Service (FIGAS)', *Falkland Islands Journal*, 1992, p. 30.
7. D. Wheeler, *The Miracle of Life* (London, c. 1935), p. 229.
8. We are indebted to Lionel Burman, Curator of Decorative Arts at the Walker Art Gallery, Liverpool, for the pottery identifications.
9. Mrs Joan Spruce of Stanley recalled the rubbish pits in the back garden and this inspired the explanation for the contents of the *Jhelum*'s hold.

CHAPTER THIRTEEN

THE STABILISATION PROGRAMME

Tim Parr's survey of 1984 established the condition of the *Jhelum* and his findings were confirmed by a second survey in January 1987. Most of his recommendations for first-aid stabilisation work were carried out in that and in subsequent visits. From the aspect of its condition the hull could be divided into four sections:

1. The hull below the water mark
2. The hull between high and low water marks – 'the splash zone'
3. The fore-hold above the high-tide mark
4. The after-hold above the high-water mark

From the absence of any apparent movement in the after end of the vessel, and the experience of other timber structures that have been totally immersed, the underwater portion of the ship was probably reasonably sound.

Section 2, the 'splash zone' had suffered deterioration since 1976 because it was alternately in and out of the water. In addition, the starboard side from the stem to the causeway had suffered from wave action, which had removed planks and eroded the structure still further. This appears to be the same problem as that which has affected most of the other wooden hulks in Stanley harbour and was probably made worse by increased shipping activity since the end of the war with Argentina in 1982.

The fore-hold above the high-water mark had suffered a steady deterioration. Because of rainwater lodging on the horizontal surfaces, pockets of rot have formed and rotten matter has accumulated like peat on the stem breasthooks. The problem was compounded because these timbers were a handy perch for local seabirds, especially night herons (*Nycticorox nycticorox* Tyaza-Guira) and shags (*Phalacrorax magellanicus*). Their droppings enriched the rotted wood and the pockets of rot in the deck beams were colonised by seeds blown off the land. The two main varieties were pearlwort (*Colobanthus quitensis*) and thrift (*Armeria macloviana*). The latter had also colonised small pockets of peaty soil between the rocks in the loading causeway. The rot also contained abundant numbers of woodlice (*Porcellio scaber* Latreille).[1] These plants helped to retain moisture in the tops of the deck beams, thus accelerating decay of the wood. As described in chapter 8, all of the forward hold beams had collapsed

The 'splash zone' in the fore-hold. The frames are vulnerable to the constant battering of the waves with the loss of the planking and the ceiling. They were colonised by a large number of mussels.

except HC. None of the main deck beams right forward were intact and the four still in place were all weakened. Once these had given way the steeply angled starboard side would have had to support itself; and as already noted its 'base' in the splash zone had already been weakened by the loss of planking and the opening up of scarphs in the framing. This framing was exposed to the full strength of the prevailing wind and waves. While this had one good effect in the sense that it kept the starboard side clear of rot and prevented lichens and other plant life from gaining a hold, it put a lot of pressure on what was in essence a large unsupported sail. There was therefore a likelihood of the whole starboard forward side collapsing into the hold. At the same time, the port forward side with the upper part of its framing was badly rotting and with much of the outer planking was spreading outwards. Sections of the forward rail had fallen off since 1978.

The after-hold section of the *Jhelum* above the high-water mark was generally in much better condition than her forward end. This was largely because of the corrugated roof and cladding. Again the port side had much more vegetation than the starboard because of its sheltered position. Large sections of its outer planking were missing. The 1983 fire had caused some damage to the starboard side of the poop though it had not fundamentally weakened that area. The worst loss was in the damage to the cabin panelling and other evidence of the accommodation. The roof sheets were rusting and many of the fixing nails were loose. It was particularly bad on the port side between main deck beams DN and DO. Their ends and those of the hold beams below them had large pockets of rot on the upper surfaces. The

The vegetation has been partly cleaned off main-deck beam DK. An eyebolt for lashing down a boat or boats is visible at the centre.

poop hold beams and carlings round the skylight were in very poor condition and were close to collapse. Water seepage had begun to affect the poop accommodation planking and also the beams supporting them.

It was clear that the rate of deterioration was increasing and that unless a first-aid programme was started much of the *Jhelum* would have collapsed within five to ten years. It was also clear that there were not the resources within Stanley or the Falklands to carry out this work. In the event it was decided that staff from Merseyside Maritime Museum would be entrusted with the task. The Museum, which was set up in 1980, and its predecessor, the maritime history department of Liverpool Museum, had taken an interest in the hulk over a number of years because of her importance to the port's own history. There had been discussions with the Falkland Islands Government about the possibility of moving all or part of the hulk back to Liverpool. The cost was confirmed as prohibitive by Tim Parr's 1984 survey. In addition to the financial, engineering and conservation problems, there was a growing feeling among the islanders that the wrecks, and particularly landmarks like the *Jhelum*, were as much a part of their heritage as the rich populations of wild life. The sale of the steel barque *Fennia* to San Francisco owners and its subsequent scrapping in Montevideo was much regretted. On the other hand, the Merseyside Maritime Museum was anxious to make as full a record of the hulk as possible and in the event was able to combine stabilisation with recording. Indeed, the first phase of stabilisation, the support of the starboard bow, was essential to safe working on the hulk.

The first-aid programme concentrated on three main targets: supporting the bow area, shoring up the starboard side, strengthening the starboard splash zone and

Starboard poop showing the damage caused by the fire of 1983.

repairing the roof. In late 1986, volunteers from the 1st Battalion, the King's Regiment, the local Liverpool regiment, mended the port side of the roof and fitted four wire ropes across the bow to hold the two sides together. They were fastened to steel plates which spread the load between two frames and were tensioned with bottle screws. The volunteers also fixed crawling boards in the bow which proved very useful for later work. The American team working on the recovery of a section of the American clipper *Snowsquall* at the East Jetty also began the treatment of some of the rotted timbers with creosote, which was available in good quantities in Stanley.

In January 1987 this work was followed up by a two-man team from the Merseyside Maritime Museum. Pine baulks measuring 6 x 6 inches were obtained from the Government Stores. One was laid between the hold stanchions to act as a fixing point and anchor for three more which were used to shore up the starboard side. The surviving fore-hold hold beam and deck beams were cleared of plant life, treated with creosote and given covers of marine ply to protect them. On the starboard splash zone the butts of the loose planking were refastened. The gaps where the planking was missing and the frames were under attack from the waves were filled in with floorboarding and plywood. Finally, the worst sections of the roof were repaired. The previous repair by the King's Regiment had not been successful because the deck planking to which it was fastened was not in good enough condition to grip the nails. This was stripped and relaid on new 2 x 3 inch bearers. Some existing sheets had corroded at one end and new half sheets were slipped in and fastened to prolong their life. The worst parts of the poop roof on the starboard side were also replaced.

This work was continued in the second visit of November to December 1987. A second phase of the first-aid programme was carried out in January 1990. The work was concentrated on the bow and the poop. The sagging deck beams of the poop were shored up by a substantial internal frame and all the corroded corrugated iron sheets were replaced. The breasthooks were cleaned down, soaked in creosote and covered with marine ply. The port-side forward timbers were also creosoted and strengthened by wooden boards. The latter were fastened on either side to produce a strengthening sandwich of new timbers to support this badly rotted area. All earlier repairs were checked and more plywood was fastened along the splash zone. The outer part of the jetty was strengthened and some of the modern rubbish and loose rotten timber and corrugated iron was cleared off the ship with the help of volunteers from the Stanley group of Operation Raleigh.

At the time of writing these works seem to be doing their job well and holding the situation. But they are not the final solution. The hull, especially the starboard bow, needs more protection from the prevailing wind and waves. More internal strengthening will be needed eventually and the port side will have to be shored up. The timbers can be felt moving under the impact of a gale. Tim Parr's proposal for a

The bracing for the poop deck beams, 1990.

Volunteers from the 1st Battalion, the King's Regiment, were responsible for setting up the wire ropes in the bow.

wave-breaking barrier beyond the bow would help to protect them. But this and indeed other long-term stabilisation proposals face twofold problems: cost and resources. There is a supply of local stone which could be purchased from the Public Works Department but the problem would then be to deliver it to the tipping zone. Wire-mesh gabions filled with stone would use less material but a shallow-draft, flat-decked craft with a crane would be needed to put them into position. Another possibility would be to demolish the existing wooden jetty and replace it with a solid stone jetty over which lorries or dumper trucks could drive their way out and across the loading port area amidships to tip stone on the starboard side. This would demand much more stone but would have the advantage of creating a permanent and safe walkway out to the hulk. This would certainly increase the interest in her and give the Falklands Museum an opportunity to establish her as a branch of Britannia House. The Stanley Maritime Trail with a panel on the *Jhelum* at the landward end of the jetty has already been set up by Falklands Tourism. But visitors would benefit from a closer view of the ship.

Such a scheme would have two drawbacks. First, it would increase the risk of casual damage to the hulk – the 1983 fire was thought to have been caused by a visitor's cigarette. Second, a solid stone causeway would substantially change the look of the *Jhelum* and the landscape of the upper harbour. Perhaps improved sheathing on the starboard side using surplus temporary road sections would be a useful interim wave-breaking measure. There would still be the cost of moving even scrap material and a method would need to be devised to anchor it in the sand and along the hull. Another desirable long-term improvement would be the installation of more internal strengthening in the fore-hold to replace the missing deck beams and covering in the whole area. This would of course change the appearance but this must be considered as essential to the long-term protection of the most vulnerable section of the hull.

All these suggestions do no more than prolong the existing situation. The protections proposed so far all depend on a structure whose fastenings are becoming looser and weaker. The ironwork, though massive, is already badly wasted. An overall hangar of the type used for the 17th-century Swedish warship *Vasa* would be an improved solution if the *Jhelum* could be left in situ. Provided the underwater hull remained sound this would give her protection and shelter for interpreting her structure. This would be expensive, though cheaper than moving the hulk ashore or salvaging her for preservation at Liverpool. At this point, the question has to be asked whether

Jim Forrester mending the roof over the stern hold. Note also the deteriorating condition of the jetty. Sulivan House is in the background. The original house owned by the Packes was burnt down in 1928 and this successor was built on the same site.

the hulk is worth preserving at that level of expense, which would run into millions. While there is no similar vessel preserved in the British Isles, the whaler *Charles W. Morgan* of 1841, which has many similarities in hull design and construction, is well preserved at Mystic Seaport Museum in the USA. There are also several British coastal merchantmen, such as the *Kathleen and May*, the *Garlandstone* and the *Emily Barratt*, which need further resources to keep them preserved. While smaller, and rigged as schooners or ketches, they are direct descendants of the *Jhelum*. They are not 8,000 miles away in the South Atlantic. The attraction of the original object is nevertheless a strong one. But the *Jhelum* does not have the pull of uniqueness, of being a technical landmark like the *Cutty Sark* or the *Great Britain*, and it is doubtful that she would attract the level of funds needed to carry out any of these final solutions.

A more realistic future would be to try to keep the hulk as intact as possible for as long as possible where she lies in Stanley. With small injections of money and labour it should be possible to roof her and protect her starboard side. In addition, plans should be drawn up to identify key sections that should be saved if and when she begins to break apart. These might include a section of the tween deck, the bow and the stern.

Notes

1.   We are grateful to Dr John Edmondson and Dr Ian Wallace of Liverpool Museum for identifying the plant and insect specimens. See also T.H. Davies and J.H. McAdam, *Wildflowers of the Falkland Islands* (Bluntisham, 1989).

CHAPTER FOURTEEN

CONCLUSION

The investigation of the *Jhelum* has filled a major gap in our knowledge of Liverpool ships and shipbuilding in the early 19th century. As far as Liverpool ships built before 1850 are concerned, Merseyside Maritime Museum's collection contains only two models – the *Watt* of 1797 and the *Sandbach* of 1828 – and no plans of sailing ships. The Whitby Museum's collection contains a plan of the whaler *Baffin* built by Mottershead and Hayes for the famous Scoresbys in 1820. The *Jhelum* was built at the end of this era and therefore adds to the sequence. The full-sized hulk is a huge repository of additional information, especially about materials, design and construction. It amplifies and illuminates surviving documentary records. The overall picture of this great fleet is well documented through records, such as the miraculously complete set of Liverpool ship registers, the local newspapers, and the Customs Bills of Entry, *Lloyd's Register* and the records of the port authority. But detail of the working of individual ships or the management of particular enterprises is rare. The extraordinary survival of the hulk of the *Jhelum* has been a catalyst for a dig into these and other sources in order to bring together a picture of how her owner-builders worked.

Steel & Co. may well prove to be typical of Liverpool and for that matter British mercantile enterprise in the middle of the 19th century. The *Jhelum* was a workhorse, not glamorous but ordinary and perhaps for that all the more important. Throughout history, the articles in common use are often those that are least recorded and the most difficult to reconstruct and yet for later generations they can equally be the objects of the greatest fascination, the things that help us make the imaginative leap back into the past, the insight that emphasises the similarities and differences with our ancestors. To give two examples: what can be more evocative than the pewter chamber pot from the wreck of Charles II's Royal Yacht *Mary* or the pathetic sailor's leather shoes from the *Mary Rose*? The hulk of the *Jhelum* is very much of that character – an everyday ship, of a type that was seen in hundreds in the ports of Victorian Britain and the Empire. Captured by early photographers like the Reverend Calvert Jones at Swansea, Samuel Smith at Wisbech or Roger Fenton in the Crimea and glamorised in the ship portraits of marine artists like the two Walters and Heard of Liverpool, the *Jhelum* acts as the pathway to understanding these two-dimensional images from the time. Similarly, when examining the documents the human dimension springs into focus. The desertions so often mentioned in the *Official Log Books* become immediately comprehensible when you have measured the space in which fourteen men lived for months on end in all weathers without heat or proper light.

It is a lucky chance that the climate of the Falklands has been conducive to the preservation of the *Jhelum* and equally that the major institutions of the Islands, the Falkland Islands Government and the Falkland Islands Company, have preserved their records. These contribute much to our understanding of the end of the final voyage. By combining records and archaeology, an all-round picture has begun to emerge of the career of one mid-19th-century sailing vessel. What is important about her is that she was ordinary. The clippers, the record breakers – *Lightning, Champion of the Seas*, etc – have been given their tribute. But essentially they were aberrations, built to serve one or two high-paying trades where speed attracted a better return. The *Jhelum* is a useful corrective. However, there is still more that could be done with her. The present investigation was carried out with the minimum number of people. A large team equipped with pumps could carry out a more extensive excavation. What is more, she is not the only Liverpool-owned hulk in the Falklands. The *Actaeon* (1838), the *Egeria* (1859) and the *William Shand* (1839) were all owned in Liverpool and their investigation might yield interesting comparisons with the *Jhelum*, especially the *Actaeon* and the *Egeria*, both Canadian-built. There is still further work to be done on the question of whether the *Jhelum* fits into the end of a local Liverpool tradition of ship design. She is not a derivative of an East Indiaman, but it would be interesting to see how she might be linked with earlier vessels and Liverpool's reputation for building 'Guineamen' at the end of the 18th century.

The *Jhelum* has a significance beyond Liverpool. As the most intact of the wooden hulks at Stanley she is an important part of the maritime heritage of the Falkland Islands. The Stanley hulks plus the *Vicar of Bray* and the *Garland* at Goose Green form the biggest concentration of 19th-century sailing ship hulks in the world. A significant number of later iron and steel merchant sailing ships have been preserved. These include the *Balclutha* (1886) at San Francisco, the *Star of India* (1863) at San Diego, the *Elissa* (1877) at Galveston, the *Wavertree* (1885) and the *Peking* (1911) at New York, *Falls of Clyde* (1878) at Honolulu, the *Belem* (1896) at Bordeaux, the *Viking* (1907) at Gothenburg, the *Af Chapman* (1888) at Stockholm, the *Passat* (1903) at Travemunde, the *Pommern* (1903) in the Aland Islands, the two Russian training ships *Kruzenshtern* (1926) and *Sedov* (1921), the *James Craig* (1874) at Sydney and the *Polly Woodside* (1885) at Melbourne. The only wooden ones actively preserved are the *Sigyn* (1887) at Abo, Finland, the *Edwin Fox* (1853) in New Zealand, and the *Charles W. Morgan* (1841) at Mystic Seaport. There is of course a wealth of material about wooden sailing ships in contemporary works such as those of Hedderwick, Richardson, Fincham, etc, and in plans such as those of the Hillhouse Collection at the National Maritime Museum and the Brocklebank Collection at Merseyside Maritime Museum. There are some good contemporary models such as those already mentioned at Liverpool, the barque *Ravensworth* (1856) in the National Maritime Museum, the ship *Claudia* (1844) and the whaler *Alice Mandell* (1851) at the Science Museum, London, the half model of the ship *William Miles* (1818) at Bristol, and the *Agnes* (1818) at Glasgow Museum of Transport. Ship portraits are also noted for their accuracy; but understanding of all these sources is enhanced by reference to the real thing. Small details that are puzzling in miniature become clear at full scale. The *Jhelum* is the 'real thing' and this was why stabilisation was given the same priority as the recording programme. Yet, it must be admitted that it will be difficult to preserve her indefinitely, and this is why the detailed record is important, for it can be studied long after the original has disintegrated and it can be reconstituted in models or, looking even further ahead, into a full-scale replica. This is not as fanciful as it may sound. A much larger replica of the 17th-century Dutch East Indiaman *Batavia* will be launched in 1992 after seven years' building at Lelystad in the Netherlands. The *Jhelum II* would certainly make a significant addition to the nation's stock of historic craft and perpetuate the memory of a ship that deserves to be famous for being ordinary.

APPENDICES

APPENDIX 1

Ships Built by Joseph Steel and Joseph Steel & Son, 1831–59

Name	Rig	Tons	Date	Owners	Classification
Joseph Steel					
Cordelia	Ship	370	14th April 1831	Taylor, Potter & Co	12A1
Imogen	–	330	26th January 1832	Taylor, Potter & Co	10A1
Thomas Leech	Brig	168	30th August 1832	Taylor, Potter & Co	10A1
Ellen German	Brig	176	1832	John Bibby	11A1
Faerie Queen	Barque	313	1833	–	–
Mary Somerville (or *Summerville*)	Ship	407	1st January 1835	Taylor, Potter & Co	–
Enterprise	Ship	338	1835	Steel & Co	7A1
Irlam	Barque	279	1836	Barton, Irlam & Higginson	–
Joseph Steel & Son					
Maid	Barque	–	23rd May 1839	J. Mondel & Captain B. Sproutz	–
Livingstone	Ship	407	1840	Taylor, Potter & Co	12A1
Buenos Ayrean	Barque	349	6th July 1840	J. Steel	12A1
Brazilian	Brig	179	1841	Job Brothers	11A1
Viscount Sandon	Ship	540	1842	Taylor, Potter & Co	
Dorisana	Ship	486	1843	J. Steel	12A1
Charlotte	Ship	535	May 1844	Barton, Irlam & Higginson	12A1
Hannah Salkeld	Ship	553	3rd April 1845	J. Steel	–
Anna Henderson	Ship	587	3rd April 1846	J. Steel	–
Zillah	Barque	342	1847	J. Steel	10A1
Helen Wallace	Ship	641	1848	J. Steel	12A1

Jhelum	Ship	466	24th May 1849	J. Steel	–
Fairfield	Ship	671	1851	J. Steel junior	–
Grand Bonny	Ship	701	1852	T. Harrison & Co	7A1
Tinto	Barque	433	1852	J. Steel	13A1
Joseph Steel	Ship	900	14th April 1854	J. Steel junior	13A1
Toftcombs	Ship	673	1856	J. Steel junior	13A1
Agra	Barque	829	9th January 1858	J. Steel junior	13A1
Rancaqua	Barque	324	1859	J. Steel junior	13A1
Mary Ellen	Brigan-tine	110	August 1859	Gladstone & Co	13A1

Sources: *Gore's Liverpool Advertiser*, except for the *Agra* which is from *Liverpool Chronicle,* and *Lloyd's Register* compiled by A. Wardle, LNRS Collection, with modifications by MKS. Note some dates are not the actual date of the launch but the date of the report of the launch, e.g., *Jhelum* launch 24th May and reported 7th June 1849.

APPENDIX 2

Register Entries for the *Jhelum* Transcribed from the Liverpool Shipping Register, Merseyside Maritime Museum

No. 173/1849

11th July 1849

Tonnage	466 $^{14}/_{100}$ tons
Launched	24th May 1849
Surveyor	William Nott
Number of Decks	one and break
Number of Masts	three
Rig	ship

Length from inner part of main stem to fore part of

Stern aloft	118.5 feet
Breadth	24.6 feet
Depth of hold amidships	17 feet

Square Stern
Woman's bust as figurehead

Shareholders

Joseph Steel the Younger, Shipbuilder of Liverpool	8
William Bell, Master Mariner of Liverpool	16
Joseph Steel Senior, Shipbuilder of Liverpool	24
Joseph Witham Coull, Master Mariner of Liverpool	16

Transactions

1st May 1852 Joseph Steel Senior sells 24 shares to Joseph Steel the Younger.

Re-registered 8th April, 1856 No. 98.

No. 98/1856

8th April 1856

Under deck tonnage	406.28
Closed in spaces –	
above tonnage deck (break)	22.07
Gross tonnage	428.35
Length 123.1 feet from fore part of stem	
to aft side of head of stern post	
Main breadth to outside plank	27.1 feet
Depth of hold from tonnage deck to	
ceiling midships	18.1 feet

Note: 27th July 1858, rig altered from ship to barque

Shareholders

Joseph Steel, shipbuilder of Liverpool	32
William Bell, Master Mariner of Liverpool	16
Joseph Witham Coull, Master Mariner of Liverpool	16

Transactions

1.   8th April 1857 J. W. Coull dies, by his will dated 5th March 1852 Joseph Steel is appointed executor. Probate is granted 10th June 1857. Transfers J.W.C.'s share to his executor J.S. Registered 14th March 1863.

2.   6th March 1863 Joseph Steel transferred 16 shares to Joseph John Coull gentleman of Liverpool, transaction Registered 14th March 1863.

3.   14th March 1863 Joseph John Coull transferred 16 shares by Bill of Sale Joseph Steel. Transaction registered 30th March 1863.

4.   Joseph Steel and William Bell sell 48 and 16 shares to Joseph Cunard James Archibald Ker Wilson, shipbrokers of Liverpool (joint owners of Bill of Sale dated 23rd March 1863). Transaction registered 24th March.

5.   Joseph Cunard and J.A.K. Wilson sell 64 shares to Matthew Isaac Wilson merchant of Liverpool. Bill of sale dated 23rd April 1863. Transaction registered 23rd May 1863.

6.   Matthew Isaac Wilson sells 32 shares to John George Widdicombe and 32 to Charles Rayley Bell, both shipowners of Liverpool. Bill of Sale dated August 1863. Transaction registered 24th August 1863.

Further entries in small Transactions book no. 13.

Transactions

1.   J. G. Widdicombe sells 11 shares to James Stannus, Master Mariner of Carrickfergus, Antrim. Bill of sale dated 21st August 1863. Transaction registered 3rd September 1863. C. R. Bell sells 10 shares to the same James Stannus on the same date.

2.   J. G. Widdicombe sells 5 shares to Robert Parry coal merchant of Liverpool. Bill of Sale dated 1st September 1863. Transaction dated 3rd September 1863. C. R. Bell sells 5 shares to said Robert Parry on the same date.

No. 351/63

4th September 1863

Transactions

1.   C. R. Bell sells 4 shares to Edwin Rabyjohn Moxey, accountant of Cardiff. Bill of sale dated 9th September 1863. Transaction dated 16th September 1863.

2.   J. G. Widdicombe sells 4 shares to William Widdicombe, Master Mariner of Cardiff. Bill of sale dated 20th August 1863. Transaction dated 22nd August 1863.

3.   J. G. Widdicombe transfers 12 shares on 16th May 1867 on security of £500 plus 10% to Carruthers Charles Johnston and John Henry Yates, gentlemen of Liverpool. Transaction registered 17th May 1867.

4.   C. R. Bell transfers 13 shares on security of the same amount to the same gentlemen on the same day.

5.   J. G. Widdicombe transfers 12 shares subject)to William Widdicombe
           to mortgage A.   ) shipowner of 4 Snowdon
) Street, Smithdown Road
6.   C. R. Bell transfers 13 shares to mortgage B.)Liverpool (formerly of
) Cardiff). Bill of Sale
7.   James Stannus transfers 21 shares.   ) dated 10th June 1869.
)Transactions registered
8.   Robert Parry transfers 10 shares.   ) 17th June 1869.
)
9.   E. R. Moxey transfers 4 shares.   )

10.   W. Widdicombe transfers 64 shares to secure £1250 plus 10% to Henry Woodall Esq., and J. H. Yates aforesaid of Liverpool, 12th June 1869. Transaction Book No. 4, p.450.

11.   W. Widdicombe transfers 64 shares to secure current account to Martin Diederich Dacker and George Offer, 115 Leadenhall Street, London, ship and insurance brokers, on 30th August 1869. Transactions registered 5th April 1870.

Ship condemned at Port Stanley 30th September 1871. Register closed 4th October 1871.

APPENDIX 3

The *Jhelum*'s Voyages, 1849–71

1849

24th May	Jhelum launched from Steel's yard, Baffin Street, Liverpool and reported in *Gore's Liverpool Advertiser*, 7th June 1849.
1st June	Entered for loading Salthouse Dock, brokers Wainwright and Lea, *Liverpool Customs Bill of Entry*, 16th June 1849.
11th July	First registry, no. 173/1849

Voyage 1

12th July	Cleared outwards for Bombay, 19 crew. W. Bell master.
16th November	Arrives at Bombay, *Lloyd's List*, 22nd December 1849, 127 days.

1850

8th January	Sails from Bombay for Liverpool, *Lloyd's List*, 20th February 1850.
17th April	Arrives at Albert Dock, Liverpool, *Lloyd's List*, 18th April 1850, and *Liverpool Customs Bill of Entry*, 17th April 1850, notes in Albert Dock, 18 men, cargo mainly cotton, myrobolams and coir, 100 days.

End of Voyage 1

Voyage 2

8th/10th June	Sails from Liverpool, Salthouse Dock, W & J Tyrer and Ashley Brothers, brokers, 18 men, W. Bell master, general cargo including

woollen and cotton textiles, wine, hard-ware, glass, tools etc. *Liverpool Customs Bills of Entry*, 3rd May-8th June 1850.

28th September   Arrives at Arica, *Lloyd's List*, 21st November 1850, 111 days.

8th November   Arrives at Islay from Arica, *Official Log Book*, also calls at Iquique to load part cargo (see *Liverpool Customs Bill of Entry*, 3rd May 1851).

1851

31st January   Sails from Islay for Liverpool, *Liverpool Customs Bill of Entry, 3rd* May 1851.

3rd May   Arrives at Liverpool, *Lloyd's List*, 5th May 1851, *Liverpool Customs Bill of Entry* notes in Albert Dock 17 men, J. Steel junior agent, cargo mainly wool, from Arica and Islay, nitrate from Iquique, copper, copper ore and barilla from Arica, 93 days.

End of Voyage 2

Voyage 3

16th May   Entered for loading for Valparaiso at Prince's Dock, Miller and Thompson, brokers, W. Bell master, *Liverpool Customs Bill of Entry*, 16th May 1851.

1st July   Cleared outwards for Valparaiso, general cargo, 20 men.

25th July   Spoken on passage 11°N 25°W, *Lloyd's List*, 20th September 1851.

20th September   Spoken on passage 56°S 66°W, *Lloyd's List*, 19th December 1851.

October   Probable arrival at Valparaiso

November–   Sails for unknown South American west coast port, probably
December   Coquimbo, for nitrates.

1852

11th January   Arrives at Valparaiso from 'Tongoy' or Coquimbo probably with guano, on passage to Baltimore, *Lloyd's List*, 6th April 1852.

10th May   Arrives at Baltimore, USA, from Coquimbo via Valparaiso, *Lloyd's List*, 28th May 1852, 121 days.

19th June   Sails from Baltimore with flour, corn, sasparilla root, wine (2 barrels) and locust wood treenails. *Liverpool Customs Bill of Entry*, 23rd July 1852.

23rd July	Arrives at Liverpool, Albert Dock, 17 men, agent. J. Steel junior. Both 19th and 23rd, *Liverpool Customs Bill of Entry*, 23rd July 1852, 35 days.

End of Voyage 3

Voyage 4

24th July	Entered for loading for Arica and Islay at Salthouse Dock, Poole & Co or Cotesworth & Co, brokers, W. Bell master, *Liverpool Customs Bill of Entry*, 24th July 1852. [n.b. it would have been days if not weeks before she discharged her cargo at Albert Dock and moved into Salthouse for receiving cargo].
27th September	Cleared outwards for Arica and Islay with general cargo, *Liverpool Customs Bill of Entry*, 28th September 1852.
28th September	Sailed from Liverpool, *Lloyd's List*, 29th September 1852.

1853

January– February	Arrived at Arica from Liverpool, *Lloyd's List*, 12th March 1853. (Reported but no date of arrival given).
24th February	Arrived at Islay from Arica, *Lloyd's List*, 5th May 1853.
22nd May	Arrived at Arica from Iquique, *Lloyd's List*, 19th July 1853.
14th July	Sails from Valparaiso for Liverpool with wool, skins, copper and tin barilla from Arica and Islay, and nitrate of soda from Iquique, *Liverpool Customs Bill of Entry*, 19th October 1853.
19th October	Arrives at Liverpool, Albert Dock, 17 men, J. Steel junior agent. *Liverpool Customs Bill of Entry*, 19th October 1853, 98 days.

End of Voyage 4

Voyage 5

6th December	Cleared outwards from Liverpool for Valparaiso, W. Bell master, *Liverpool Customs Bill of Entry*, 6th December 1853.

1854

11th March	Arrives at Valparaiso from Liverpool, *Lloyd's List*, 2nd May 1854, 96 days.

6th May	Severely damaged in hurricane at Valparaiso, *Lloyd's List*, 29th June 1854.
27th July	Sails from Valparaiso to Iquique, probably to load nitrates, *Lloyd's List*, 19th September 1854.
21st August	Arrives at Iquique from Valparaiso, *Lloyd's List*, 5th October 1854.

1855

27th February	Arrives at Liverpool from Islay, *Lloyd's List*, 1st March 1855.

End of Voyage 5

Voyage 6

13th April	Sails from Liverpool to Valparaiso, W. Bell master, *Lloyd's List*, 14th April 1855.
24th July	Arrives at Valparaiso from Liverpool, *Lloyd's List*, 19th September 1855, 103 days.
8th September	Arrives at Valparaiso from Iquique, *Lloyd's List*, 31st October 1855.
9th October	Sails from Mejillones for Liverpool with wool, hides, sheepskins, brazil wood, nitrate of soda from Islay and nitrate of soda from Mejillones, *Liverpool Customs Bill of Entry*, 29th January 1856.

1856

29th January	Arrives at Liverpool from Mejillones and Islay, Albert Dock, 19 men, J. Steel agent, *Liverpool Customs Bill of Entry*, 29th January 1856, for both the above. [n.b. call at Valparaiso probably for orders or to clear customs] 113 days.

End of Voyage 6

Voyage 7

31st January	Entered for loading for Valparaiso, Prince's Dock, *Liverpool Customs Bill of Entry*, 31st January 1856.
8th April	Re-registered at Liverpool 98/1856.
14th April .	Cleared outwards for Valparaiso from Salthouse Dock, 12 men, J. Poole & Co. and Imrie & Co., brokers, W. Crawford master, *Liverpool Customs Bill of Entry*, 14th April 1856.

| 17th April | Sails from Liverpool for Valparaiso, *Lloyd's List*, 18th April 1856. |

| Late July–
  mid August | Arrives at Valparaiso from Liverpool, *Lloyd's List Index*, 4th October 1856, refers column 19, and mentions Valparaiso. Reference not found in *Lloyd's List*. |

| Late December | At Iquique, *Lloyd's List Index*, 3rd or 8th February 1857 refers column 9, reference not found in *Lloyd's List*. |

1857

| 2nd January | Spoken 40°S 89°W Valparaiso for London referred to as 'Ghelume' *Lloyd's List*, 18th March 1858. |

| 30th March | Arrives at London from Islay with wool, bark, saltpetre, copper, sheepskins and oxhides. *London Customs Bill of Entry*, 30th March 1857. |

End of Voyage 7

Voyage 8

| 7–10th June | Sails from London to Valparaiso, W. Crawford master, *Lloyd's List*, 10th June 1857, and Official Log Book. |

| 5th October | Arrives at Valparaiso, *Official Log Book*, 117 days. |

| 19th November | Sails from Valparaiso for Coquimbo, *Lloyd's List*, 22nd January 1858. |

| 4th December | Arrives at Coquimbo, *Official Log Book*. |

| ? December | Sails from Coquimbo for Caldera. |

| 9th December | Arrives at Caldera, *Official Log Book*. |

1858

| Mid-January | Sails from Caldera for Hamburg, probably with copper or copper ore. |

| 25th April | Reported at Deal, on passage for Hamburg, *Lloyd's List*, 26th April 1858. |

| 27th April | Arrives at Cuxhaven on passage for Hamburg, *Lloyd's List*, 1st May 1858. |

| 2nd June | Sails from Hamburg for Liverpool with spirits, spelter, old metal, flour, peas, beans and one case of toys, *Liverpool Customs Bill of Entry*, 14th June 1858. |
| 14th June | Arrives at Liverpool, Albert Dock, 16 crew, J. Steel agent, *Liverpool Customs Bill of Entry*, 14th June 1858, 12 days. |

End of Voyage 8

Voyage 9

23rd June	Entered for loading for Valparaiso, Salthouse Dock, J. Poole & Co., brokers, J. Seymour master, *Liverpool Customs Bill of Entry*, 5th July 1858.
27th July	Converted to barque, *Liverpool Ship Register*.
29th July	Cleared outwards and sailed from Liverpool for Valparaiso. *Liverpool Customs Bill of Entry*, 29th July 1858 and *Lloyd's List*, 31st July 1858.
24th August	Spoken, 12°N 26°W, *Lloyd's List*, 28th September 1858.
28th August	Spoken 11°N 23°W, *Lloyd's List*, 7th October 1858.
20th November	Arrives at Valparaiso from Liverpool, *Lloyd's List*, 20th January 1859 [n.b. *Official Log Book and Crew List* implies 1st December 1858], 115 days.
29th December	Sails from Valparaiso for Iquique, *Official Log Book* [n.b. referred to as 'Piqnidanque'].

1859

1st January	Sails for Cobija, *Lloyd's List*, 4th March 1859.
14th February	At Iquique loading copper ore, *Official Log Book*.
1st March	Sailed from Iquique for Liverpool with 500 tons of guano, *Liverpool Customs Bill of Entry*, 23rd June 1859.
23rd June	Arrived at Liverpool, Queens Dock, 14 men, J. Steel agent, *Liverpool Customs Bill of Entry*, 23rd June 1859, 117 days.

End of Voyage 9

Voyage 10

27th July — Entered for loading for Valparaiso, George's Dock, G.H. Fletcher & Co. brokers, J. Seymour master. *Liverpool Customs Bill of Entry*, 29th July 1859.

7th September — Cleared outwards from Liverpool for Valparaiso, *Liverpool Customs Bill of Entry*, 7th September 1859.

12th September — Sails from Liverpool, *Official Log Book*.

27th December — Arrives at Valparaiso from Liverpool, *Lloyd's List*, 17th February 1860, 107 days.

1860

7th January — Sails from Valparaiso for Huanillo [note, 29th January, *Liverpool Customs Bill of Entry* notes 16 bales of wool loaded at Valparaiso and also loaded 636 tons copper ore at Cobija].

16th February — Arrives at Huanillo.

12th March — Sails for Liverpool.

28th June — Arrives at Liverpool, 15 men, Queen's Dock, J. Steel agent. All three entries above from *Official Log Book*, *Lloyd's List* and *Liverpool Customs Bill of Entry*, 29th June 1860. [n.b. discrepancy between *Official Log Book* and *Bill of Entry* on cargo loading ports], 109 days.

End of Voyage 10

Voyage 11

10th July — Entered for loading for Guayaquil at Princes Dock, G.H. Fletcher & Co., brokers, A. Garrioch master, *Liverpool Customs Bill of Entry*, 29th July 1860.

20th August — Cleared outwards for Guayaquil, general cargo, 16 men, *Liverpool Customs Bill of Entry*, 20th August 1860.

9th October — Spoken 16°S 45°W, *Lloyd's List*, 3rd December 1860.

18th December — Arrived at Guayaquil from Liverpool, *Lloyd's List*, 31st January 1861, 121 days.

1861

25th January   Thomas Rodger, carpenter, drowned at Guayaquil, *Official Log Book.*

4/5th February   Sails from Guayaquil for London, with tobacco, india rubber, orchella weed and cocoa, *Official Log Book* and *Lloyd's List*, 2nd April 1861, and *London Customs Bill of Entry*, 22nd May 1861.

22nd May   Arrives at Gravesend, *Lloyd's List*, 22nd May 1861, 108 days.

End of Voyage 11

Voyage 12

12th June   Sails from London for Swansea, A. Garrioch master, *Official Log Book.*

29th June   Sails from Swansea for Valparaiso, probably with coal. *Lloyd's List*, 29th June 1861.

7th October   Arrives from Swansea at Valparaiso, 100 days.

10th October   Sails for Coquimbo, this and 7th October, *Lloyd's List*, 28th November 1861.

11th December   Sails from Coquimbo for Liverpool, probably with nitrate of soda, *Official Log Book.*

1862

28th March   Arrives at Liverpool from Coquimbo, *Official Log Book*, 109 days.

End of Voyage 12

Voyage 13

17th May   Sails from Liverpool for Valparaiso, A. Garrioch master, *Official Log Book.*

19th June   Spoken 5°N 27°W, *Lloyd's List*, 29th July 1862.

20th June   Spoken 4°N 25°W, *Lloyd's List*, 16th August 1862.

29th August   Arrived at Valparaiso from Liverpool, *Lloyd's List*, 14th October 1862, 105 days.

4th October	Arrived at 'Tortonillo', *Lloyd's List*, 3rd December 1862 and sailed for Iquique.
5th November	Sailed for Liverpool via Mejillones, *Lloyd's List*, 2nd February 1862.

1863

22nd February	Arrives at Liverpool from Iquique and Mejillones, *Official Log Book*, 110 days.

End of Voyage 13

23rd March	J. Steel & Co sell the *Jhelum* to Cunard and Wilson, *Liverpool Ship Register*.
23rd April	Cunard and Wilson sell the *Jhelum* to Matthew Isaac Wilson, *Liverpool Ship Register*.
25th May – 9th July	Survey and repairs carried out at Liverpool, *Lloyd's Survey Report* No. 18262.
24th August	Matthew Isaac Wilson sells the *Jhelum* to John George Widdicombe and Charles Rayley Bell of Liverpool.

Voyage 14

22nd August	Sails from Liverpool to load at Newport for Buenos Aires and Callao, J. Stannus master, *Lloyd's List*, 25th August 1863.
16th September	Sails from Newport (probably with coal) for Buenos Aires, *Lloyd's List*, 18th September 1863.
30th November	Arrives at Buenos Aires, from Newport, *Lloyd's List*, 19th January 1864, 76 days.

1864

2nd April	Sails from Buenos Aires for Callao and the Chincha Islands in ballast to load guano. *Official Log Book* noted three replacements signed on.
29th July	Arrives at Callao. *Official Log Book*, 109 days.
7th October	Arrives at Callao from the Chincha Islands (presumably loaded with guano), *Lloyd's List*, 16th November 1864.

13th October   Sails from Callao for Barbadoes, *Lloyd's List*, 29th November 1864.

4th December   Arrives at Barbadoes from Callao, *Lloyd's List*, 30th January 1865, 54 days.

1865

25th March   At St Jago de Cuba, *Official Log Book*.

12th April   Probably sails for Swansea, *Official Log Book*.

27th May   Arrives from St Jago de Cuba, probably with copper ore at Swansea, *Lloyd's List*, 28th May 1865.

End of Voyage 14

Voyage 15

26th June   Sails from Swansea for Bahia, J. Stannus master, *Lloyd's List*, 27th June 1865.

31st August   Arrives at Bahia from Swansea, *Lloyd's List*, 2nd October 1865, 67 days.

9th October   Arrives at Pernambuco from Bahia, *Official Log Book*.

10th October   Sails from Pernambuco to Paraiba, *Official Log Book*.

16th November   Sails from Paraiba for Liverpool with cotton and old iron, *Liverpool Customs Bill of Entry*, 15th February 1866.

1866

15th February   Arrives at Liverpool, at George's Dock, 14 men, Widdicombe and Bell agents, *Liverpool Customs Bill of Entry*, 15th February 1866, 93 days.

End of Voyage 15

Voyage 16

14th February   Sails from Liverpool to Vera Cruz, J. Stannus master, *Official Log Book*.

22nd July   At Vera Cruz, date of arrival not known, Bernard Quinn, cook, killed, *Official Log Book*.

July/August   Sails for Tupilco from Vera Cruz for mahogany logs, *London Customs Bill of Entry*, 2nd November 1866.

July/August   Sails for London via Havannah.

7th September   Sails for Havannah for London, *Official Log Book*.

2nd November   Arrives at London, *Official Log Book*.

End of Voyage 16

30th November–   Lloyd's survey after dry-docking for repairs.
  13th December

1867

Voyage 17

5th February   Sails from London for Rio de Janeiro, J. Stannus master, *Official Log Book*.

11th February   Reported off Deal, *Lloyd's List*, 12th February 1867.

15th February   Reported off Falmouth, *Lloyd's List*, 16th February 1867.

2nd May   Arrives at Rio de Janeiro from London, *Official Log Book*, 87 days.

1st July   Sails from Rio to Tabasco for orders to load mahogany at Tupilco, *Official Log Book*.

21st July   Spoken 9°N 43°W on passage Rio to Tabasco, *Lloyd's List*, 24th August 1867.

1st September   Sails from Tupilco to London, *Official Log Book*.

12th December   Arrives at London, *Official Log Book*, with mahogany logs, *London Customs Bill of Entry*, 16th December 1867, 103 days.

End of Voyage 17

1868

Voyage 18

3rd January   Sails from London to Cardiff (presumably in ballast), J. Stannus master, *Official Log Book*.

25th January	Arrives at Cardiff, *Official Log Book*, 23 days.
13th/15th February	Sails from Cardiff for Buenos Aires, probably with coal, *Official Log Book*.
12th June	Arrives at Buenos Aires, *Official Log Book*, 119 or 117 days.
4th/6th August	Sailed from Buenos Aires to Callao, probably in ballast, *Official Log Book*, *Lloyd's List*, 17th September 1868.
3rd October	Arrives at Callao, *Lloyd's List*, 13th November 1868, noted as a casualty but no detail, 61 days.
13th October	Sails from Callao to the Chincha Islands, *Lloyd's List*, 27th November 1868.
25th November	Loading at the Chincha Islands with 29 other vessels, all for French ports including 9 for Dunkirk, *Lloyd's List*, 2nd January 1869.
7th December	Sails from the Chincha Islands with guano for Dunkirk, *Official Log Book*, [n.b. *Lloyd's List*, 13th January 1869, gives 10th December as sailing date].
16th December	Sails from Callao [presumably called to clear outwards], *Lloyd's List*, 27th January 1869.

1869

23rd April	Arrives at Dunkirk from Callao, *Official Log Book*, *Lloyd's List*, 27th April 1869, 129 days.

End of Voyage 18

10th June	Sold to William Widdicombe, *Liverpool Ship Register*.

Voyage 19

26th June	Sails from Cardiff, probably with coal for Montevideo, J. Beaglehole master, *Official Log Book*, *Lloyd's List*, 30th June 1869.
22nd July	Spoken 14°N 28°W, *Lloyd's List*, 26th August 1869.
25th July	Spoken 11°N 27°W, *Lloyd's List*, 6th September 1869.

20th September	Calls at Rio de Janeiro, 'leaky', *Lloyd's List*, 21st October 1869. [n.b. *Official Log Book* notes two men sent ashore to hospital on 22nd September 1869], 87 days.
19th October	Sails from Rio de Janeiro for Montevideo, *Lloyd's List*, 18th November 1869.
13th November	Arrives at Montevideo, *Official Log Book*, 31 days.
18th November	Sails for Rosario, *Official Log Book*.
11th December	Arrives at Rosario, *Official Log Book*.

1870

8th February	Arrives at Montevideo from Rosario, *Lloyd's List*, 14th April 1870.
8th/9th March	Sails for Callao, probably in ballast, *Official Log Book*.
18th April	Arrives at Callao from Montevideo, *Lloyd's List*, 27th May 1870, 42 or 43 days.
22nd April	Sails from Callao for Guanape Islands for guano, *Lloyd's List*, 1st June 1870.
April–May	Dates unspecified, vessels loading at Guanape Islands reported in *Lloyd's List*, 16th June, 21 loading (including *Jhelum*, 18 for France, 8 for Dunkirk). 1st August, 39 loading, 31 loading for France.
6th July	Arrives at Callao from Guanape Islands, *Lloyd's List*, 15th August 1870.
12th July	Sails from Callao for Dunkirk, *Official Log Book*.
18th August	Arrives at Stanley, Falkland Islands, 'leaky with jettison', 'surveyed three times, master undecided as to what course he should adopt' *Lloyd's List*, 29th October 1870, *Official Log Book* and *Governor's Despatches, FIG archives*, 38 days.
27th December	Report from Le Havre of charter of barque *Pelham* to load *Jhelum*'s cargo, *Lloyd's List*, 27th December 1870.

1871

11th January	Salvage Association reported *Pelham* loading *Jhelum*'s cargo and will sail in 10 days. *Lloyd's List*, 22nd March 1871.

2nd March	Officers of HMS *Galatea* survey the *Jhelum* at the request of the Governor, *FIG Archives, Inward Correspondence*, also reported in *Lloyd's List*, 21st April 1871 and it was understood that the report 'is of a condemnatory nature'.
25th April	*Pelham* arrives at Dunkirk with *Jhelum*'s cargo, *Lloyd's List*, 27th April 1871.
13th May	Captain Beaglehole signs power of attorney assigning responsibility for *Jhelum* to Dean & Co. *Official Log Book.*
27th May	Captain Beaglehole's last entry in *Official Log Book*, taking passage to England on HMS *Charybdis*.

APPENDIX 4

The Form of Charter-Party Adopted by Messrs I. Thomson, T. Bonar & Co., the English Agents of the Peruvian Guano Consignment Company

LONDON,   18

It is hereby mutually agreed between   Owners of the tons   register new measurement, on the one part, and Messrs. I. THOMSON, T. BONAR & Co., of London, for and as Agents of the Guano Consignment Company of Great Britain (the charterers), for the Supreme Government of Peru, on the other part as follows:-

That the said vessel now   shall sail direct, after discharging outward cargo, to Callao, where the captain shall immediately place the ship at the disposal of the said Guano Consignment Company advising them in writing.

That the said vessel on inspection by the appointed officer, being then approved as tight, staunch, strong, and well-conditioned for the voyage, the charterers shall (within forty-eight hours after such report being received) send to the captain or his agents, orders for loading a cargo of guano at the Chincha Islands, to which place the vessel shall at once, proceed, calling on her way at Pisco, to obtain the necessary pass to load, which shall be given to the captain by the charterers' agents, free of expense, within twenty-four hours of his application.

After completing her loading of guano, and having obtained the necessary pass from Pisco, the vessel shall return for her final clearance to Callao, where the captain shall have the liberty of taking in passengers, light goods, and specie, on freight for the benefit of the ship. The charterers to have the option of shipping the light goods at current rates.

The ship when laden, shall not go through the Boqueron Passage, between the Island of San Lorenzo and the Main Land.

The ship shall convey from Callao to the Islands, any specie that may be required for the payment of the cargo, and any tools (sent alongside by the charterers whilst the vessel is at anchor in Callao), free of freight: and shall supply, free of charge, either on board or alongside, at the Guano Ports, any water that may be required by the charterers, not exceeding one per cent. of the register tonnage.

At the Chincha Islands the vessel to be placed under the Mangueras to load, or at the option of the charterers' agent there, the cargo to be placed in the ship's boats, and in them conveyed on board at the ship's expense and shipper's risk.

Such sacks as shall be supplied by the charterers at their discretion, shall be filled with guano, and the mouth of the sack sewn up at owner's expense, the charterers providing twine, and the sacks shall be used for lining the vessel.

The owners to find necessary dunnage, and to be responsible for damage by negligence.

The owners to be liable for all damage arising from side lights or ports.

The guano shall be stowed so that a clear space may be left around the vessel, under the deck, for the purpose of examining the cargo, and removing any water which may have been shipped; and every convenient opportunity shall be taken to examine the guano, and means used to prevent and lessen damage.

The quantity of guano to be shipped shall not exceed one-third above the vessel's register tonnage, new measurement, except with the consent in writing of the charterers' agent at Callao, and which consent the charterers undertake shall be given to all ships which their agents have not fair and reasonable grounds for believing to be overloaded, when such consent may be withheld, and if any vessel proceed to sea without such written consent, and loss should be sustained by the charterers upon the guano, and whether the same be of a nature of a particular or general average, or of charges upon the guano, all such loss as between the said owners and charterers shall be deemed to have arisen from the improper loading of the vessel, and the amount of such loss shall be borne and paid by the said owners to the said charterers; but in the case of loss in the nature of particular average, the owners shall only pay to the charterers such amount as may exceed £3 per cent. upon the net value of the limited cargo of guano hereby agreed to be shipped.

No guano or other dead-weight shall be received on board except by order of the charterers or their agents.

Should political or other circumstances prevent there being sufficient labourers at the loading-place, as many of the crew as shall not be absolutely necessary for the safety of the ship, shall be sent on shore to load the cargo, they receiving the usual labourer's daily pay while so employed.

Ten running days (Sundays excepted) for each one hundred tons, new register measurement, to be allowed the charterers for loading the ship at the Islands, nevertheless in no case shall the charterers have less than thirty, nor more than eighty such days in all. Said days to commence from the day the master gives notice, in writing, of being ready to receive and take on board, and to cease when the charters' agents give notice that the vessel may leave the Islands.

Thirty days to be allowed the owners for taking in light freight and specie as above specified.

Over and above the lay-days allowed the charterers for loading the ship, and to the owners for taking in light freight and specie, each party shall be permitted to detain the vessel for those purposes respectively, for thirty days, the charterers paying to the owners, or the owners paying to the charterers, as the case may be, at the rate of £1 for every 100 register tons per day, as agreed compensation for such detention, payable in Lima at the exchange of 48d. per dollar currency.

Should the vessel be unnecessarily detained at any other period of the voyage, such detention to be paid for by the party delinquent to the party observant, at the above-named rate of demurrage or compensation.

The owners of the vessel to pay all port charges, and the ship to be consigned to the charterers (the Guano Consignment Company to Great Britain), in Lima, to whom the customary commissions and agencies for doing the ship's business shall be paid by the owners.

The captain to sign bills of lading at such rate of freight as charterers may direct, and without prejudice to this charter-party.

The said vessel shall, after completing her loading as before-mentioned proceed as ordered by bills of lading to CORK or CROOKHAVEN, (and where she is to remain until the return of post from London) for orders from the Guano Consignment Company to Great Britain, or their agents, to proceed to a safe port in the UNITED KINGDOM, unless ordered by bills of lading to proceed direct to any port and there according to bills of lading and charter party, deliver the cargo, which is to be discharged and taken from alongside, at the rate of not less than thirty-five tons per working day.

Should the charterers or their agents require that the discharge of the guano be made in sacks, they shall furnish the captain with the required number, and with threads sew them at their expense, and the owners of the ship will cause them to be filled and sewn up and delivered overside at ship's expense.

The freight under this charter-party to be paid in manner hereinafter mentioned, is at the rate of sterling, in full, per ton of 20 cwt. net weight of guano, at the Queen's beam, subject however to a deduction for the water contained in damaged guano, and on the sweepings and stones they shall only pay half-freight.

The master to be supplied in Lima with a sum not exceeding £   free of interest and commission, but the cost of insurance to be borne by the owners, and the amount so advanced, and the cost of the insurance there shall be in part payment of the freight at the exchange of 42 pence per dollar currency. And should the charterers or their agents think it necessary to advance the master beyond the said sum of £   any sum for repairs, stores, and other disbursements whatsoever, such sums, with interest, commission, and insurance, shall be in part payment of the freight, at the exchange aforesaid. And it is hereby expressly agreed, that the receipt of the master for any such sum or sums of money as shall be supplied or advanced to him by the charterers as aforesaid, shall be conclusive and binding upon the owners and their assigns, and they shall thereby be prevented as between them and the charterers from enquiry into the necessity for, or the appropriation of the sum of money which in such receipt or receipts shall be acknowledged to have been received: and all contributions to general average losses, which (if any) shall become payable in respect of any such advances as aforesaid, shall be borne and paid by the owners.

The freight to be paid (subject to the terms and conditions of this charter-party) in manner following, that is to say £1 per ton on the estimated cargo, in cash, on arrival at port of discharge, three months' interest at the rate of £5 per cent. per annum being deducted, and the balance, after deducting all such sums of money as shall become payable to the charterers or their agents under the provisions herein contained, forty-eight hours after the true and right delivery of the whole of the cargo, in cash, less three months' interest at £5 per cent. per annum, or at the option of Messrs. I. THOMSON, T. BONAR & Co., by their acceptances at three months' date payable in London, and the captain or owners shall give, in exchange for said acceptances or cash, duplicate receipts in full of all demands whatsoever upon the cargo or otherwise.

And in the event of any rival claims to the said freight, the charterers shall be at liberty to retain the same in their hands until the right of the respective claimants is determined, or to pay into court deducting their costs.

The charterers are hereby authorised to retain and deduct from the freight all claims, damages, and sums of money, as well liquidated as unliquidated, to which the owners shall become liable to the charterers, by virtue of, or in anywise in relation to this charter-party, and all seamen's wages, pilotage, and port charges, if any, which they may be compelled to pay in order to prevent the arrest thereof, it being the intention of the parties, that all claims and demands, of whatever nature, which shall accrue to the said charterers, shall be treated as payments made by the charterers on account of freight.

And if the vessel should be compelled to put into any port or ports along the Pacific or Atlantic coasts, the captain shall consign her to the Guano Consignment Company, or their correspondents; in either place paying the usual commission; such correspondents in ports of Chili being Messrs.

In VALPARAISO	Messrs. RUIZ BROTHERS
In MONTE VIDEO	Messrs. BATES, STOKES & CO.
In RIO DE JANEIRO	Messrs. EWBANK, SCHMIDT & CO.

Penalty for non-performance of this charter-party, the estimated amount of freight.

The act of GOD, the Queen's enemies, fire and all and every dangers and accidents of the seas, rivers and navigation, of whatever nature and kind soever, during the said voyage, always excepted.

The ship to be consigned to the Company, or to their agents in Great Britain, to whom is to be paid an address commission of two and a half per cent. at the port of discharge, and who are to have the right to name the docks in which the ship is to be discharged, and the broker who is to report the ship at the custom-house, and do the ship's business.

A commission of two and a half per cent. is due by the ship on signing this charter, which shall be deducted from the freight on arrival, and if the ship do not arrive at her destination, said commission shall be paid in London by the owners.

 For the Guano Consignment Co.   As Agents

Witness to the signature of Messrs. I. THOMSON, T. BONAR & Co.

Witness to the signature of

Source: R.W. Stevens, *On the Stowage of Ships and their Cargoes* (London and Plymouth, 7th edn, 1893), pp. 291–9.

APPENDIX 5

General Instructions to Masters (Liverpool)

DEAR SIR, – Having appointed you to the command of the . . . we would call your attention to the following and annexed suggestions, with a view to your maintaining good discipline on board, and pursuing the business of your vessel with energy, and exercising careful economy in regard to her disbursements:-

Keep your ship clean and in good order. When you see a proper opportunity ask to be reported, as you have MARRYAT'S signals on board.

In running down the trades, you will as usual shift your sails, repairing such as require it; the same may apply to your homeward passage, as all sails have to be repaired on board. On arrival at your port of discharge, never neglect to note your protest immediately. Then make arrangements for discharging your cargo, and give notice when ready to do so.

Hold a survey on your hatches before opening them, and at the same time get a certificate of survey from the surveyor; for should it so happen that any cargo turns out damaged, and you have not obtained such certificate, it may cost considerably more, and occasion far more difficulty to get than it would otherwise.

Should any cargo be damaged get a certificate to that effect as above.

Get receipts for all your cargo at time of delivery.

Having discharged outward cargo, give notice, in writing, of being ready to load homeward cargo. On the expiration of your lay-days, give notice in writing of same (inserting a copy thereof in ship's log-book), and then claim demurrage.

Should your claim for demurrage not be paid before sailing, get your charter-party endorsed as to the number of days occupied in loading, and if the consignee refuses to do so, go to the British consul, or a notary, and note a protest of his refusal.

Always get copies of your protests and surveys.

Should you engage cargo at one port and have to fill up at others, you must, before signing bills of lading at first port, insert the clause of 'via such and such port or ports,' neglect of this will make the ship liable for all losses consequent on a deviation from the direct voyage from port of loading to port of discharge.

Never go out of a ship's direct course to gratify any curiosity to have a look at a place in passing.

In case of ship being open for charter, and you should not, on your arrival, find letters enclosing homeward charter, do not appear to be over anxious about a freight, but state that you expect instructions from your owners by next mail, and in the meantime make yourself thoroughly acquainted with every thing offering in the freight market. However much you may desire to return to one port in preference to another, conceal your wishes on this point, as otherwise by your openly stating a particular wish to your consignee to return to London or Liverpool rather than any other port, may and very frequently does, occasion a considerable loss to the ship. Always endeavour to keep consignment of vessel open in this country.

Write fully by every available opportunity, and never omit to send copies of disbursements, accounts, protests, surveys, charter-parties, etc, etc. Name the date of ship's arrival and departure from each place. When in the United Kingdom write every second day.

IN FIXING SHIP. 1st. Take care to have stamped charters and bills of lading. They can be got stamped within 14 days after date, without payment of any penalty, and at the head office in London, within one month after date on payment of £10 penalty. After a month they cannot be got stamped at all.

2nd. Let no charterer sign as agent unless he states for whom he is agent. A man of straw, or a foreigner, may be the principal.

3rd. When a foreigner is the principal, try to get the agent in England, who effects the charter, to make himself liable as principal, and to sign the charter without adding the word agent.

4th. If freight is not payable in cash on delivery, take care that the bills are to be 'approved bills', and not charterer's bills, as in the latter case, the shipowner cannot hold the cargo for his freight, even though the charterer was notoriously insolvent. If a charterer objects to the stipulation for 'approved bills', he is generally not safe and his charter should not be taken.

5th. In stating days allowed the merchant, it is proper to say 'running days' or 'working days', according to the intention. In London 'days' mean 'working days', and Sundays and holidays do not count until the ship is on demurrage. After that time all days count.

6th. In bills of lading of a ship to consignees in England from consignors abroad, have a clause inserted – 'consignees paying freight and demurrage', if you wish to have a remedy for your demurrage.

IN LOADING. 1st. Enter the ship at the custom-house. The days count from entry at the custom-house and being ready to load.

2nd. It is however proper to give notice to the merchant, of arrival and being ready to load; and it is generally better to do this in writing, as it is more easily proved in case of need.

3rd. Enter in the log-book the day of arrival at the port of loading and entering at the custom-house. Also enter a copy of the notice given to the merchant. Also enter in the log-book the day loading is completed.

N.B. The signature of the master to the entries in the log, as well as that of the mate is very useful in case of dispute. If the master be owner or part owner, the entries should be signed by the mate, and the second mate, carpenter or eldest apprentice.

4th. If the merchant's correspondent abroad is willing to give a certificate on the back of the charter or bill of lading, of the correct number of days expended in loading, get him to do so but do not on any account allow him to certify a smaller number of days than were really spent. Rather do without his certificate as it is not at all necessary to have it.

5th. In case the merchant's correspondent at port of loading should refuse to furnish a cargo, the master should, on the expiration of the lay days allowed by charter, protest against the merchant, and he is then at liberty to return in ballast to his chartered port of discharge, and has a right to his full freight. The better plan, however, is to take the best freight he can get for his chartered port of discharge, and claim the deficiency of the freight from the merchant. It is improper to wait the demurrage days, unless required to do so by the merchant.

IN DISCHARGING 1st. Enter ship at custom-house.

2nd. Give notice to merchant of being ready to unload.

3rd. Make similar entries in the log-book of entering ship at custom-house, of notice given to the merchant, and of the day the discharging is completed, and let them be signed as before directed in the case of loading, by the master and mate, or if the master be an owner, then by the mate, and the second mate, carpenter, or eldest apprentice.

4th. If you are chartered, but have signed bills of lading, to a consignee, before you part with the cargo, the consignee should produce the endorsed bill of lading. He should also undertake for payment of freight according to bills of lading, particularly if you have any doubt of your charterer's solvency.

It is doubted whether the owner of a *Chartered* ship can recover his freight from a consignee who has once got hold of the cargo, without giving any express undertaking to pay; and it is said the only remedy is against the *charterer*.

N.B. You cannot hold the cargo for demurrage, and only for freight in terms of charter-party or bill of lading.

Source: R.W. Stevens, *On the Stowage of Ships and their Cargoes* (London and Plymouth, 7th edn, 1893), pp. 291–9.

APPENDIX 6

Survey of the *Jhelum* Conducted by J.H. Bradley, Staff Commander and R. East, Carpenter of HMS *Galatea*, 2nd March 1871

2nd March 1871 To Captain, HRH Duke of Edinburgh
HMS Galatea, Port Stanley

'Sir,

We the undersigned have been on board the British Barque 'Jhelum' now lying in Stanley Harbour and have held a strict survey of the ship and find as follows:–

The outside planking is generally defective in the butts and in their iron fastenings. The treenails are all slack and can be started out and in with a slight blow and we conclude from what we can see above the sheathing that the ship is the same below it, and requires entire re-fastening which would [require] new treenails and iron bolts as also general caulking.

Inside the ship we find the upper iron breasthook broken in the way of the throat bolt and therefore useless, both wooden breasthooks are decayed and should be removed. The tail ends of the knightheads are rotten as also the fore cant timbers. Many timbers fore and aft are decayed and are broken and much given way in the scarphs. The iron stanchions fore and aft in the hold are bent and started in their fastenings and appear too weak for their work which has caused the upper deck to sink in the waist and under the poop which latter had caused the cant pieces of the break of the poop to give way.

The hood ends of the upper deck forward are decayed and would need new shifts of plank and the upper deck generally requires caulking. The bulwarks require general repair having been washed away in places and all the iron work on the upper deck requires examining.

Two main hatchway upper deck beams are broken and require replacing.

To render the ship seaworthy we consider that the repairs of the above defects should be carried out.

We found 42 inches of water in the well and were told the ship had not been pumped out for a week.

With regard to the expense of repairing the ship or whether she is worth it we cannot form a correct judgement as we are not acquainted with the capabilities for repairs of ships in Port Stanley or the price of labour and materials.

We have the honour to be your royal highness' most obedient servants.

J.H. Bradley   Staff Commander
R. East Carpenter'

Source: Falkland Islands Government Archives, Inward Correspondence.

PLANS